BREEZE FOR A BARGEMAN

By the same author

A Slice of Suffolk. Terence Dalton
Rough and Tumble. Mallard Reprints
Coasting Bargemaster. Mallard Reprints
Last of the Sailormen. Sampson Lowe and Marston

BREEZE FOR A BARGEMAN

by

BOB ROBERTS

TERENCE DALTON LIMITED
LAVENHAM · SUFFOLK
1981

Published by
TERENCE DALTON LIMITED

ISBN 0 86138 007 X

First edition 1981
Second edition 1990

Text photoset in 11/12pt Garamond

Printed in Great Britain at
The Lavenham Press Limited, Lavenham, Suffolk

Contents

This book is dedicated to my wife and shipmate Sheila; and to the late Mrs June Dalton for her help and encouragement in the publication of my books.

Index of Illustrations

A breeze for a Bargeman.

CHAPTER ONE

"Storm Force Ten"

WEATHER-BOUND in Yarmouth — there never was a coasting bargeman who had not watched the clouds from the deck of his craft moored at the quay, wondering and hoping for a shift of wind. Like many another I had often walked down to the sea front and gazed at the white horses and flying clouds which could keep us prisoner for weeks at a time. Such was the case one November day in 1962 when the mulie barge *Cambria*, but lately discharged of her cargo of wheat up-river at Norwich, received orders to proceed to London with all speed to load 150 tons of cattle cake in the Victoria Dock. It was a good freight and we needed the work. Flat bottomed, lee-board, sailing barges cannot put up with all weathers like the round bottomed trawlers. Bargemen have to pick the right weather for a passage and make a dash for it, especially in wintertime. Moreover our mainsail was getting old and doubtful in spite of the patient repairs and patching by Everard's old sailmaker, the late Alf Naylor, at Greenhithe. I had indented for a new mainsail some weeks before and the worthy Alf was to have it ready when we reached London. The *Cambria* was owned by the Everard family of shipowners who had built up a huge fleet of motor coasters from a humble start with wooden sailing barges. And they never stinted their craft for good gear.

The weather was bad enough, but doubts about the mainsail made our gloom all the worse. Periodically the broad Scottish voice of our agent, a native of Grangemouth, would hail us from the cabin hatch.

"Are you therrre, skipperrr. London have been on the phone again about this carrrgo of cattle-cake. What arrre ye're chances?" He knew better than to urge us to get to sea, as some agents might do. Captains "ordered" to sea by shore agents generally exploded into a squall of bad language. I knew one well-known Home Trade skipper who, when disturbed by the agent knocking on his door, used to bawl out "----- off" (literal translation of which would be "go away"). Customs officers got the same treatment, and eventually brokers' runners, officials and chandlers were afraid to go near him unless they were sure he was in a good mood. They learned that when the wind and tide served he would sail anyway. And woe-betide them if they didn't have his papers ready!

Our brawny Scotsman had been aboard twice and I invited him down into our snug little cabin, where the polished panelling and bright brass cheered

Cambria heads seaward from Tilbury loaded for Norwich.

what was my home for much of the year. The mate, a lanky lad from London whose crop of red hair had got him the name of "Ginger" Latham, poured him out a pint mug of tea, amply laced with several spoonfuls of condensed milk and sugar. Just as he was about to drink it there came a screeching and a roaring as the barge, loftily rigged to eighty feet above the deck, heeled over and shot his tea across the table.

"Christ, what's that?" he exclaimed.

"Wind," I said, "and we're moored in harbour with all canvas stowed snug."

He seemed impressed. I drained his tea off the table back into his mug. He looked at it dubiously.

"Well, there goes my tea."

"You've only lost half of it. I've saved enough for half a mug. Can't waste it. The table's clean."

He gulped it down. "I take it ye'll not be sailin' today?"

"This wind's got to veer first and fine away northerly."

That night the wind did fall away a little. The lulls were more frequent. We glued our ears to the ageing radio set. The batteries were getting low but we managed to catch a faint voice saying "Wind north west, force eight, moderating to force seven and veering north-north-west." We turned in, full of hope, and I was on deck before the crack of day. The clouds were still scudding hell-bent from the west and the rising sun showed angry streaks of red between the packed cumulus.

No sooner did we tuck into breakfast than the inevitable Scottish voice came down the cabin hatch. "Did ye hear the forecast? What d'ye think of it?"

We waited for the eight o'clock radio forecast and it was the same as it had been at midnight "veering nor-nor-west." It took me an hour to make up my mind, by which time the last of the ebb was running out of the harbour and the flood tide flowing southwards and into the Thames Estuary. With a bit of luck we could be in London the next day and save that cargo of cattle cake so urgently required. It was a twenty hours passage at the most, even less. I have sailed it in fifteen, but in better weather than we had this day. An empty barge in a heavy sea bangs down like hitting the water with a frying pan. In fact, a schoonerman once said to me "I don't know how you get a thing like that about. It's only a frying pan with a rudder." He was astonished that we had made a bad-weather passage to the Humber while his ship was lying weatherbound.

The agent watched anxiously as I paced the deck. So did the mate. If the wind came out north-north-west we could make our passage however hard it blew. We could hold the Suffolk shore round Orfordness and gain some shelter from the half-tide sandbanks of the Estuary. *Cambria* was a good sea-barge — as good as many a round bottom ketch.

"All right. Order the tug."

The agent was ashore like a flash. Ginger got the tow-rope crossed so that it led out of the port fairlead and was made fast on the starboard bollards, which is the proper sailorman's method of towing in rough weather and strong tides. Ginger had become a good mate over the years. He had started life as a clerk in a London insurance office — hated it — longed to go to sea. He joined me as a raw hand and through sheer determination, patience and hard work had made himself into a seaman and was proud to be classed as one. At the time of writing he is the certificated captain of a handy 500 ton motor ship, carrying cargoes between English and Continental ports. "In bad weather I treat her like a barge," he once said to me after "tacking" his ship across heavy seas over the North Hinder bank.

Our tug was the little service boat *Stalker*, but she had quite enough power to tow a light barge. Her skipper, an ex-fisherman, knew the cross-tides at Yarmouth Pierheads, where the frothy whirlpools had caused damage and death to many a vessel trying to get in or out. Experienced coasting masters used to say that the worst harbours to "take" on the East Coast were Seaham and Yarmouth.

When the worthy *Stalker* came ponk-ponking alongside I specially asked her skipper to be on the alert should we have to return to harbour, and, being a good seaman himself, he grimaced skywards and said he would keep a lookout for us.

In our anxieties about the weather I almost forgot that there was a third person aboard us — a passenger who had always dreamed of making a passage in a sailing barge. Not being a seaman, he was delighted that at last we were making a start.

Down the long harbour we went, everything lashed down for a rough passage and the topsail, which we were not likely to need, tightly stowed aloft. Ginger had learned that with two strong gaskets round the topsail a bargeman could sleep more soundly than depending on double clewlines or a riverman's stow.

Once outside the pierheads we let go the tow close to Gorleston beach to keep under the lee of the land. The tug crew shouted "Good Luck" and waved us farewell. I glanced astern and saw them having a bit of a struggle to get back into the harbour. The wind was blowing a full gale from west-north-west. The *Cambria*, leaning on her port leeboard, ramped along boldly round Lowestoft Ness and up through the narrow Covehithe channel, past my mother's birth-place at Kessingland.

Hopes were high until we were off Southwold. Then it suddenly became very dark, although it was only late afternoon. The white lighthouse in the middle of the town was completely blotted out. It seemed as if someone had thrown a blanket over our heads. It was a snowstorm, black as the ace of spades and bitterly cold. Within minutes of the onslaught there was a rending and ripping sound near the mainmast and I saw a great chunk of our sail flying away in the darkness like some magic carpet. It was a whole cloth, two feet wide and about thirty feet long. Piece after piece tore away and there was nothing we could do about it. A few bits of mainsail hung on between the wire headrope and the leech, but to all intents and purposes the whole sail had disintegrated.

Desperately I tried to keep the barge under the land but she sagged off so rapidly that in order to control the steering at all I had to let her come off the wind and gallop seaward with the seas abeam. Ginger stood on the lee side of the wheel and I shouted to him — I had to shout to make him hear although he was only three or four feet away from me — "What price this nor-nor-west wind fining away? It's backing south-west now and blowing all the harder." It was force ten, I learned later from Suffolk coastguards, gusting eleven at times.

There was nothing to be done except keep the seas abeam or on the quarter for safety's sake and pray for a patch of better weather and a northerly slant.

As the mainsail was ripped to pieces we were forced to tackle the problem of saving the spars. The seas were steep and curled over in a white froth as they swept down on us, the hollows between them a mass of wind-driven spume. There was no canvas left to hold steady our 62 foot pitch pine sprit. To the uninitiated this is a huge spar which holds out the peak of the mainsail and is slung by the heel from the hounds aloft to a heavy iron collar and chain round the main mast near the deck. It could drive down through the barge like a battering ram if it got adrift.

We called up our passenger to help. The vangs and vang falls were jerking to and fro like giant whips, threatening to break shackle pins and tackles at any moment and land us in disaster. We would founder and drown because in such seas rescue would have been both improbable and impossible.

While I hung onto the wheel Ginger watched his chance to get a momentarily slack tackle fall onto the barrel of a leeboard winch. With the aid of a safety stopper, and with the help of the passenger, who was a cool headed chap, Ginger got three turns on the winch barrel and hove the lee vang tight. This partially steadied the wildly snatching spar until they could heave the weather vang in. It was no mean feat in the semi-darkness. We got a bowsing rope across the deck from one vang to the other and at last I felt some relief from

Cambria in Dunkirk after the storm had ripped her mainsail to pieces.

Tattered remains of *Cambria*'s mainsail.

one of our several anxieties. At least the spars would not come crashing down on top of us.

As night fell the darkness was accentuated by snow and sleet which drove across our deck almost horizontally at times. We were wet and cold.

"There's a light! What's that?" Ginger had spotted it in spite of his bad sight and snow blown spectacles. I took a quick glance to leeward.

"It's the bloody Gabbard. We're driving to leeward like a bladder of lard."

I kept the the foresail full and was able to hold the barge about six points off the wind so that she was going ahead at about two knots and sideways about three. We were too far off to seaward to hope for any shelter from the Kent coast or the Goodwin sands. A few ships passed within a couple of miles or so but none came near and we did not flare for assistance. I had in my mind the times of the tide and calculated that by daylight we might feel the benefit of the west-going flood.

Ginger earned my everlasting gratitude by miraculously producing a cup of tea and cutting some inch thick cheese sandwiches. This certainly gave us new heart. Our gallant passenger was not interested in any form of refreshment. Periodically he popped his head out of the cabin hatch, had a little puke, and disappeared below again. There was nothing he could do to help anyway. The

6

next light we saw was the Galloper and still there was not the slightest let up in the weather. The warnings on the radio were still "North West force 10", but there wasn't much north in it for us. It was mostly West-by-North. The Sandettie light loomed up and I told Ginger that he was about to make a foreign voyage.

"Where to?" he asked.

"According to how we come into the tide along the Flemish banks, it will be Dunkirk, Ostend or the Scheldt". Fortunately I had got to know that coastline fairly well over the past forty years, although I had no chart aboard of the modern lights and buoys.

Our battle with the elements made the hours of darkness seem to pass quickly. I was too cold to be tired and too wet to be cold. The salt spray which had reached my underclothes was warmed by the heat of my body.

Just before daylight we saw a dipping row of lights. It was the Continental shore. The seas were so heavy that at first they looked like flashing lights as the crests hid them and we dropped in the hollows. Whatever place it was, we were to windward of it. But it was a dangerous lee shore. Ginger looked at me anxiously.

"What do you reckon?"

"We're about to join the Common Market", was all I could say. Occasionally we saw a big flashing beacon ashore but it was impossible to count the flashes owing to the high seas. It could be either Dunkirk or Ostend. According to my mental reckoning the tide was making to the south-west. Suddenly, as daylight came, we both saw something that made our hearts leap with joy. It was the great grey hump of the Dunkirk steelworks — a mark we immediately recognised from our trip across for the twenty-fifth anniversary celebrations of the wartime evacuation of the troops from the Dunkirk beaches to which the *Cambria* had been invited the previous June.

"It's Dunkirk! All's well. We'll be in the Cafe Flandria tonight, with a bit of luck, having a glass with Raymond Chaumorcel."

I could now allow the barge to come off the wind a bit further and she started to ramp ahead and give us better steerage way. The water on the off-shore sandbank was menacing and boiling white. I had Ginger on the lead line because we had to chance our luck across the low-way to the west of the harbour. We drew three feet six inches.

Three fathoms — three fathoms again — we were entering the white water now. Two fathoms — two again — less a quarter — fathom and a half — two — two — two and a half — four. We were over. I bore up for the harbour mole. The northwest gale was still whistling through the rigging but I knew now that we had won. We surged into the entrance and tore up the long harbour like a destroyer. No one hailed or hindered us. Up past the dock gates we ran.

"Down foresail — stand by your anchor."

Ginger had the sail off in a trice and unrove the shank painter from the anchor.

"Let go."

We chucked round on our anchor close to the fish quay, dredged alongside, got a rope ashore and we were berthed. A little group of French fishermen came along and stared at the flapping remains of our mainsail.

Our passenger helped us moor and clear up the debris to the accompaniment of pints of hot tea. Then he sat down on the hatches and, instead of being joyful at our survival from the storm, looked melancholy and serious. Sadly he said to me, "I've got to send a telegram to my wife".

"Well," I said "You will be able to tell her you are safe and sound in a good harbour."

"It's not that" he said, rather mournfully. "For years she's been on at me about having a holiday in France and I've always said we can't afford it. Now I've got to tell her I've arrived in France. I hope she'll understand."

Ginger gave me a meaningful glance and shrugged his shoulders. "Whatever happens, you can't please everybody."

We had not been moored at Dunkirk Fish quay for more than a couple of hours before we found a friend on hand. A British motor barge came chugging alongside and who should it be but young Jack Whiting from Chatham, Master of the *Horation*, trading regularly to Dunkirk. He was one of an old Kentish barge family.

"I saw you come up the harbour. I shall be back here in a few days, Bob. If your owners can have a mainsail ready, I'll bring it over to you and if your passenger wants to get home, I'll take him with me as soon as this weather eases." He called up Everard's Greenhithe office on his radio.

Our luck was surely in. True to his word, Jack picked up the *Sara's* racing mainsail in London and after being held up by more gales finally dropped it on our deck a week later.

The French fishermen and longshore folk were very interested to see Ginger and me strike our forty three foot topmast, stay the thirty-eight foot bowsprit, and lower the mast down by means of the fore stayfall on the windlass. We unbent the remnants of the mainsail which hung about the rigging like streamers. The handiest tool for this job was a sharp knife. The onlookers were even more interested to see the fresh sail bent while the spars and rigging were down. The little crowd on the quay grew larger each day as most of the fishing fleet were weather bound in harbour.

"Now," they said "how are you going to get it all up again? No cranes here. You will need some men to help." I explained how the job was to be done in my "English French". I waved my hands in horror when the word "crane" was mentioned.

"nous heavons sur le windlass — clinkety clonk. Very strong windlass — tres forte. Et les mast and la voil arrive a haute", pointing upwards. They understood. How many men to heave it all up? I let them confer and guess. Ten men, they said, would be needed.

I shrugged my shoulders like they did and slowly shook my head. They continued to shrug their shoulders and paced up and down, gesturing and argueing among themselves. I thought it was time to cut their argument short. It made a bit of fun, anyway.

"O.K. En France — dix hommes. En Angleterre — deux." Ten fingers followed by two fingers rubbed in my point. I had been told as an infant by our village school master that one Englishman was worth ten Frenchmen. At least I was giving them the benefit of one extra Englishman.

Ginger and I manned the windlass handles in a "We'll show 'em" frame of mind. Foot by foot the mast, sprit, sail and rigging crept higher until it was half way up and we could ship the short handle and get the windlass pawls rattling to a merrier tune than the slow clonk clonk of the heartbreaking initial heave. Up topmast, with the heel wire on the mast case winch, on stopper, and we were ready for sea.

The gales howled on for a few more days and being almost out of funds, we lived on herrings, camembert cheese and French bread. Occasionally we had a glass of wine with my old friend Raymond Chaumorcel at the Cafe Flandria. It had been rebuilt after the destruction of the town by the Germans, but years before I had frequented the old place when his mother kept it. Raymond was a bluff friendly French man with, I suspect, a deal of Flemish blood in his veins as

M.V. *Horation*, Captain Jack Whiting, comes alongside *Cambria* in Dunkirk to offer assistance.

had many others along this coast. Once he invited us to Sunday dinner: and what a dinner! It lasted from one o'clock to half past four, with rabbit meat, garnished and beautifully cooked in several different ways by his Bordeaux wife, different wine for each course and liqueurs to finish up with. In the field of cooking, I take my hat off to the French, and to Madame Chaumorcel in particular. For flavour, delicacy and satisfaction, one French meal is worth ten English ones!

One day, a French shipping agent paid us a friendly visit and brought his eighty year old father aboard. Down in the cabin, the old man, who spoke good English, recalled his days before the first world war when he had been agent for fleets of English sailing barges trading to and from Dunkirk.

"They were fine vessels, beautifully kept with varnished spars and gold leafed scrolls and always in spotless condition. The Captains were quite rich gentlemen in their way, but if you upset one of them he would punch you on the nose. They wore bowler hats, leather jackets and thick 'fearnought' trousers."

While we were waiting for the weather to ease I found another Chatham motor barge loading tiles in the dock. Her master was the late "Old" Jack Whiting and I went aboard for the pleasure of a yarn in my own language. We talked over-long into the night until I glanced at his old alarm clock on the mantel shelf over the cabin fire.

"Good lord, Jack. I did not realise it was as late as that. Is that G.M.T. or Central European Time?"

It could be said that Jack's reply was that of a very insular Englishman who had never traded abroad until he was sixty.

"I don't care a sod what time they say it is here. That's the time by Chatham Town Hall, and I put it right when I left."

One night there was a deathly calm — a change in the weather. And in the morning came a sweet little draft from the south west. Just as it was getting daylight, the *Cambria* slipped quietly out to sea with the *Sara's* white racing main sail drawing beautifully.

Cambria's cargo book reads:—

November 29	Sailed light from Yarmouth for London.
November 30	Sheltered from stress of weather and loss of mainsail in Dunkirk.
December 12	Sailed light from Dunkirk.
December 18	Arrived London.
December 20-21	Loaded 150 tons ground nut cake ex s.s. *Mergui*, Tilbury Dock for Bunn's Wharf, Yarmouth.
December 23	Arrived Yarmouth.

Above. *Veronica*, sailed by Jack Nunn, chasing the *Sara*.

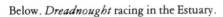

Below. *Dreadnought* racing in the Estuary.

An old-time racer, the *James Piper*. Note the square rigged ships in the Thames Estuary.

CHAPTER TWO

Farm Boy To Top Skipper

IT WAS back to the same old grind — the Yarmouth trade. Sailing barges had for many years taken cargoes out of big ocean-going ships in London for the Yarmouth and Norwich merchants. Everard barges were the most frequent arrivals in Yarmouth, winter or summer, and their masters used to say with sarcasm that if you saw an Essex barge in Yarmouth you knew it was summertime. But one bargemaster in the Everard fleet was originally an Essexman and he was always regarded, and respected, as the "top-skipper". His name was Jim Mole of East Mersea and he told me that he started life as a farm boy on the island at five shillings a week (twentyfive pence in modern coinage). But there was more money to be earned in a barge. He got ten shillings a week and his food in an old coaster working the North Sea and Channel ports.

Jim grew up to be the complete sailorman. He carried his sails into almost every port in the North Sea and Channel and across to the Continent and Channel Islands. Everard could boast of some of the finest coasting bargemasters in the heyday of their craft. Apart from Jimmy Mole, there was Jesse Farthing from Harkstead in Suffolk, Frank Day from Gravesend and Tom Willis of Greenhithe, who later settled at Belton in Norfolk. Many of the later up-and-coming skippers learned a lot from these men, who were not the sort to flaunt brass buttons and boast of their prowess. Jimmy Mole's "uniform" for as long as I can remember him was a battered trilby hat, braces and carpet slippers in summer, plus an old jacket and jersey in winter. It was he who induced me to take the "boomie" *Martinet* (210 tons) in the Channel and East Coast trade before the second World War.

"You're just the chap they want for her" he said. "You've been master in schooners and ketches and this old *Martinet* is almost the same rig as you were in as a lad."

In later years it was a joy to watch Jimmy Mole and Jesse Farthing fitting out the famous *Sara* for the barge races which took place in the Thames and Medway. These two elderly gentlemen, who were old friends over many years of seafaring, going quietly round the deck each doing some essential piece of rigging which the other would never even look at or question. Such was their faith in each other's knowledge and ability. Few words were spoken. Then they would stop, look at each other and nod. That meant "Time for a pint". And

Sara racing in the Thames Estuary. 86 feet long, drawing only two and a half feet of water, she is carrying 5,850 square feet of canvas. Her ''bob'' (masthead house flag) is 80 feet above the deck.

they were always first barge to be ready for trials. I sailed with Jimmy in the *Sara* and sometimes we could get Tom Willis to help us when he could be spared from his motor ship. When the barge races were revived in the Coronation Year of 1953, the *Sara* was the only entrant to be given an extensive and expensive preparation. Some thirty Everard yard hands worked aboard her and Jimmy Mole was recruited to sail as mainsheetman, on whose judgement the man at the wheel has to rely implicitly, especially in close quarters. She could not help winning, whoever had sailed her, because all the others in the race competed with scratch gear raked out from pre-war days. *Sara* walked away from them all at the very start and came home some two miles ahead. But it was really a hollow victory. In later years, against the modernised *Sirdar* and *Veronica*, she had to fight for every foot of the forty-eight mile course and was beaten.

Of the three crack barges, the *Veronica*, originally built at Greenwich in 1906 and rebuilt from almost a wreck by Everards, proved the fastest. The Ipswich built *Sirdar*, launched in 1898, represented the London and Rochester Trading Company and the *Sara*, which was a product of White's yard in Conyer Creek, Kent in 1902, had to battle for second place.

Barge race day was always in late spring or summer and there was a grandeur about these shallow, flat bottomed craft of little over a hundred tons, drawing only two foot six of water, carrying as much as 6,000 square feet of canvas, with 43 foot topmasts, 49 foot mainmasts, a sprit of 66 feet and 45 foot bowsprits. They needed *real* sailormen.

When the men able to handle this much gear in all winds became hard to find, the Barge Race Trust was wound up in 1963. That was the end of 100 years of real barge racing. Amateurs later bought up old craft and had a bit of a race each year, but it was not the same as in the hell-for-leather days of skippers like Jimmy Mole, Jack Nunn of Greenhithe and Tom Cook of Halstow. Jack Nunn, who thrashed the lot of us with his flying favourite *Veronica*, was the son of "Old" Jack Nunn, one of the best racing skippers Everard ever had, who had once won in the little *Princess*. "Old" Jack lived and thought racing from one year's end to another. I sailed with him once when he was short of a mate and my barge was under repair after we had been machine-gunned in the war. Although I had been a barge-master for many years I learned something from his every move when we came down river in company with a Kentish rival named the *Surge*. Both barges had delivered cargoes of cement in the Royal Albert Dock. The *Princess* was last out of the lock and I saw Jack's gaze fixed on the barge ahead.

Rochester's pride — the *Sirdar*.

"Reckon you can catch her, Jack?" I said.

He stroked his long white moustaches and nodded "Presently".

Gradually we drew up close astern of the *Surge*, so named because the letters meant "Sure you are *Giralda's* equal". *Giralda* was a famous racing champion of years gone by. The wind headed us in Long Reach which stretches from some three miles from Purfleet to Greenhithe. Jack had me constantly trimming sheets and vang falls a few inches here and there. The *Surge* had the weather berth and her skipper was artful enough to keep it. Two tacks and Jack said:

"Bob, we'll sail through her lee. You'll have to jump about and I'll show you how it can be done. It might come in handy for you when you go racing or want to get by another barge to beat her for turn."

While I held the wheel, he put a slippery knot in the slack of the mainsheet. Then he told me stand by the weather vang, which controls the peak of the mainsail. Jack luffed the *Princess* under the *Surge's* stern. The *Surge* luffed in reply to bar us from getting to windward. Both barges then filled away again. A second time Jack luffed and the same performance was gone through as before.

"Now stand by that vang fall, Bob. Ready?"

Jack luffed again but not so hard as before, just enough to let the foresail give a single kick. The *Surge* luffed hard again, his sails ashake.

"Now — slack your vang — quick — that'll do — hold it." The sprit swayed away to leeward and Jack ran to the mainsheet and let it fly until his slip-knot stopped in the upper block. In a matter of seconds the *Princess* was freed off the wind and darted ahead ramping full. Jack pulled the helm up as quickly as he could get the spokes round. Down helm again.

"In sheet — quick — now get that vang in under his lee."

The *Surge* was still ashake as we ramped past to leeward, coming on the wind as I hove frantically to get the *Princess's* gear close-hauled. Having lost a deal of speed by luffing ashake, the *Surge* was slow in bearing up and by the time she was full-and-by again we were past her and clear. Jack winded again and the *Surge* had to wind under our lee.

"Shove the kettle on, Bob. We've got time for a cup of tea now." The *Surge* dropped only a length astern of us, but she never caught up again.

Mistley bargemen from up the Stour used to be very keen on racing and some of them were very good at it. Several times they took championship cups back to their little home port, and among them 'Fat Nobby' Finch was the craftiest helmsman who ever held a racer's wheel. He lies in Mistley churchyard, and as I watched his coffin lowered into the grave, a barge chap near me muttered "Nobby's luffed himself ashore at last." With him went a skill and knowledge that is gone forever. It was the same with the passing of old Jack Nunn.

Top skipper Jimmy Mole.

Centenarian Dick the Dagger watching the last of the real barge races when the Match Trust was
wound up in 1963 after 100 years of racing.

CHAPTER THREE

Hard Days

THE hardest barge sailing of all, despite the summer races, was done by the coasters in rough weather and on dark winter nights — down to the Humber and King's Lynn, to dangerous silting ports like Wells in Norfolk, down-Channel with cement for Exeter, cattle food for Poole, linseed to Northam and up the shallow Medina to Newport in the Isle of Wight. Pick the wrong time of tide to arrive and the wrong sort of weather for that particular port, and a barge could be lost with all hands. Coasting barges sometimes had to crack on every inch of sail to get to a destination at the right time to enter, or to beat another barge for first turn to unload, or maybe stand out to sea and heave-to until conditions were suitable to take the port. Tom Willis in the 285 ton *Ethel Everard* once had to run past the mouth of the Humber, were he was bound, because of the spring ebb and mighty seas breaking across the shallows, and spent two and a half days hove-to off Flamborough Head until the weather moderated sufficiently for him to beat south again and enter the Humber. Tom was a fine sailorman, strong as an ox and honest as the day is long. He had been mate with Jimmy Mole in his young days, trading to the Continent and Channel Islands in flat old barges like the *Her Majesty*, which had about as much sheer as as a painter's plank. In later years crews would not take the *Her Majesty* outside the Port of London limits. Tom was decorated for the part he played in the evacuation of Dunkirk by the Allied Armies. He took over supplies and dynamite for the Royal Engineers to blow up abandoned equipment and beached his lovely *Ethel Everard*, of which he was so proud, under intense fire from enemy aircraft. In that murderous engagement his barge was set on fire. "I could have got her off," he told me, "but the Navy would not let me stay." I suspect that was the nearest tough old Tom had been to tears.

When he came back from the Buckingham Palace investiture I asked him what the Queen had said to him. He said: "She seemed to know more about me than I knew about myself. Without any notes she asked about all my sons at sea. I've never met such a charming person in my life."

Another splendid bargeman who lived to be over a hundred years of age won an M.B.E. at Dunkirk. This was bluff old Dick Miller from Margate — always known as Dick the Dagger from his boyhood days. Apparently his

The Author leading his crew aboard the *Royal Sovereign* to receive the *Dreadnought*'s championship award.

skipper had once said: "That boy Dick is as sharp as a dagger," and the nickname had stuck to him for the rest of his life.

Dick went up to the Palace in his best jersey and a new cap (no brass buttons for him.) "The King shook hands with me and I said 'How do?'; and he said 'Well done, Skipper.' He was a fine looking chap — looked a proper King."

His barge was the *Royalty*, and she ended her days in the Dunkirk battle. Dick and his mate ferried troops out to the waiting warships in his small boat, taking a few at a time across the shallows.

I could always sit in his cabin and listen to him talking about his early days in the Margate hoy-barges, sailing to a time schedule twice a week from London with general supplies for the town. There was some hard and daring sailing done then which some of the modern racing experts would not have relished.

He started at the age of eleven in barges belonging to a Mr Keep, who owned the Greenhithe Yard before it was purchased by the original Frederick T. Everard. When a barge named the *City of London* was being sent to a Paris Exhibition in 1889, his Guv'nor said: "We must take young Dick out of that barge. Paris is a wicked City. He can go mate with young Sonny Westbrook in that little stumpy. She's only 70 tons and doesn't earn enough for Sonny to get a proper mate. Dick's had a bit of experience as third hand running stone and cement up to the Pool for building Tower Bridge. Sonny's only eighteen but he's got all the makings of a good skipper. We'll see how he and Dagger get on."

So Sonny, aged seventeen, was skipper and young Dagger, aged eleven, was mate. And they traded skillfully up and down the crowded London River with materials for building the new bridge — cement, stone, bricks and shingle. In London, Dagger told me, his skipper would not let him go ashore "Because Jack the Ripper was about and had done one in not far away from the wharf." To Sonny, Dick was always "the boy", and many, many years later, when they had grown to old age and retired, they used to come to watch the barge races. Bill and Fred Everard always saw to it that they were adequately wined and dined aboard the committee ship, *Royal Sovereign*.

One day I clambered aboard the *Sovereign* for the prize giving after winning the staysail class championship with the 160 ton *Dreadnought*. Sonny, now 95 years of age, greeted me with the words: "Seen young Dagger anywhere. I have to keep an eye on that boy or he'll get lost in this crowd."

Of course, Dick was six years younger, only 89 at the time. But to Sonny he was still the eleven-year-old nipper he had as mate when he was an 17-year-old skipper.

When Dick reached the age of 100 he was interviewed by a B.B.C. man who asked if the old chap went down to the river sometimes to look at the old barges and especially the last of them, my *Cambria*, in which he had raced as a young man.

"See 'em? — I don't want to see none of 'em any more." Which rather surprised the romantic minded interviewer! Barges to Dagger meant nothing more than a lot of hard work and sleepless nights.

Sonny died at Northfleet when he was over 95 and I talked to him a fortnight before he "let go his anchor for the last time," to use his own words. He was mentally as lively as ever and told me about his first barge race in the *Vectis*.

"We used to start from our anchors off Erith," he said. "There was an enormous crowd of us and just after the start our bowsprit got foul of the mizzen rigging of the barge just ahead of us. I wanted to show what a smart lad I was and nipped out along the bowsprit to clear it. To my surprise a chap in the other barge climbed the mizzen rigging and punched me on the nose."

If these two splendid old characters sailed into the Hereafter, no doubt Sonny would tell the boy: "Nip forrard on the quick and sing out to them to open them lock gates." And Dagger's booming voice would soon rouse St Peter into action.

CHAPTER FOUR

Trawler Navigation

NAVIGATION by the old-time fishermen and seamen was very different from the methods used today. They had no Radar, echo-sounders, auto-pilots, Decca system, or even charts in some vessels. But the masters and mates knew the waters of the North Sea and Channel as surely as a landlubber knows his way home from work.

Their main asset was a keen and incessant observation, an art lost to many men today who venture out from the shore. The modern skipper spends many hours in his bunk, on leave ashore, enjoying long week-ends at home. He cannot be part and parcel of the salt water on which he earns his livelihood, as were his fore-fathers. Just as a child's education used to be based on the "three R's" (reading, writing and arithmetic) so the old seaman was trained in the three "L's" — lead line and look-out. The lead-line was not only used to find out the depth of water, but also to gauge leeway, set and drift and speed "over the ground" in tidal waters. A lead armed with tallow would also give the mariner a sample of the bottom which would help him judge the position of a ship. An echo-sounder won't do that.

One Sunday lunchtime, "Coddy" Polly, skipper of the barge *Beric*, sat in the *Butt and Oyster Inn* at Pin Mill, surrounded by a number of yachtsmen and yachtswomen, as well as a few shore-type holiday makers. They regarded him as a "character" and treated him as some sort of curio instead of a splendid Suffolk bargeman. He was a massive man, with bright blue eyes and gold earrings and a great sense of rough humour. Shore-people didn't mean much to him but if they didn't mind his language — well laced with ancient Anglo Saxon four letter words — they could listen to many a merry tale of life in the barges and excursions ashore. When one of the admiring ladies from a large and expensive yacht asked him how he found his way about at night in the dark, unlit and often un-buoyed creeks of Suffolk, Essex and Kent, he replied that, if in doubt, he relied upon his lead line.

"And do you arm your lead with tallow, Skipper?" she asked.

"Tallow? Christ, no — s--t, — anything'll stick to s--t!"

Some laughed openly: some looked shocked. Some menfolk took their ladies to another part of the bar. But Coddy was Coddy, and you had to take him as you found him. We bargemen always found him the best of company in a four-ale bar or sitting on the main horse of a barge at anchor.

One day he was anchored at the "Stoneheaps" off Shotley when a young single-handed yachtsman came down the river Orwell and manoevred close to Coddy's barge to anchor. Being alone, he shook his craft up into the wind, hurriedly leapt out of the cockpit, dropped the foresail and let go the anchor. Alas, the chain caught round his foot and he went over with it. Fortunately, he disentangled himself and came spluttering to the surface to grab the barge's quarterboard just where Coddy was resting his broad backside. Coddy looked over the side and regarded his wet and breathless visitor with a mild curiosity.

"Been down to hook it in?"

This brief remark of many years ago must have done the rounds of every yacht club on the East Coast. Coddy died after he was made to retire ashore on grounds of old-age. For a time he used to walk down from his house to Ipswich Dock each morning as though he was going to sea, but he soon faded away. To every one who knew him he remains a memory of a stalwart worth-while man in a worth-while world — a bit of old England.

But lead line navigation in tidal creeks and estuaries is very different from an ancient method employed by the hardy Shetlanders who used to venture as much as sixty miles out into the Atlantic in open boats. Few people knew how they found their way out to distant fishing grounds and then home again to a safe landfall. They had neither chart nor compass. Frank Carr, one time Director of the Maritime Museum, making a diligent research of native Shetland craft, inquired about traditional navigation skills from the present day fishermen with modern equipment. He was directed to an ancient mariner who knew the old ways.

"We steered by the moder dye." he said.

Whichever way the wind blows, he told Frank, there is always a "mother sea" from which you can gauge your proper course. "Watch for the moder dye and you can find your way out and home." It does not always run with the wind-sea. Perhaps the Vikings knew something of the "moder dye."

My father, who was brought up in a house overlooking Liverpool River, told me of a full-rigged ship with the unfortunate name of *Dudhope* (built at Scotstoun in 1894 and owned by the Ship Dudhope Company of Liverpool.) She came up through the Bay of Biscay, bound to London after a long and hazardous voyage and encountered three weeks of northerly storms without any chance to sight of the sun or stars to fix her position. To and fro she tacked, week after week, often well out into the Atlantic to avoid getting embayed. At last, with the aid of the deep-sea lead, she slammed into the Western Approaches, every man searching the horizon for a sight of land so that they could fix their position. Then came the welcome cry from aloft — "Land-ho, Isle of Wight." The afterguard agreed that at last they had made the Wight and the ship was run off to confirm the land-fall. Soon, they thought, they would

The last "boomie" barge, the 210 ton *Martinet*, in which the author traded to East and South coast ports. She was a casualty in 1941.

pick up the southern shores of England. Visability over the Island improved until they could see it clearly through a break in the clouds.

It was Lundy Island in the Bristol Channel!

She discharged her cargo in Liverpool. With a name like that and a company also carrying the title "Dudhope" — what better could they expect.

Deep sea navigators in the Elizabethan era of discovery were often doubtful about their longitude but they were always careful to make sure of their latitude by a simple calculation from the sun's height at noon. For latitude, no chronometer is required, not even a clock of any sort, if you are patient enough to watch the sun rise to its zenith. So in Drake's day captains would get on to the latitude of their destination while well to windward of it and then run due west until they saw it.

When I sailed the 27 foot *Thelma* across the Atlantic in the North-east trade wind, my companion was an ex-policeman named Arthur Bull. Looking at a small scale chart of the Atlantic Ocean which showed the American Continent from Canada down to Cape Horn, he said: "As far as I can see, if we steer west, we can't miss it." And that is what we did, setting out from Teneriffe and arriving in Demerara River fifty days later. I wrote a book about it. That voyage, extending into the Pacific, where small, remote islands called for a more exact form of celestial navigation than the primitive, slap-happy methods I had learned from rough and ready skippers in the North Sea and Channel trade.

North Sea fishermen were never renowned for meticulous navigation. The accurate fixing of the vessel's position was secondary to finding fish. A passenger in a sailing trawler out of Lowestoft, being a contributor to a magazine, once asked the skipper what his position was. The worthy master pulled out a small-scale, grubby chart of the North Sea which showed both the British and Continental coasts. Placing a large horny hand over the position marked ''North Sea'', his thumb on the Norfolk Coast and his little finger on the Frisian Islands, he announced firmly: ''That's where we are — *there*.''

Occasionally sailing trawlers from the Dogger Bank, running homeward with an easterly wind and uncertain how far north or south they were, would miss their port and get piled up on a lee shore. This led to the Board of Trade insisting that fishing skippers should sit for a certificate, and particularly to satisfy the examiners that they could use a sextant and calculate latitude. This is a simple sum and chronometer readings and logarithms are not necessary. Any intelligent schoolboy, once shown the usage of a sextant, could work out a latitude.

But the old fishing skippers did not like the idea at all. It was quite foreign to the way they had been brought up. When an old Whitstable skipper named Harry Tapp presented himself for examination, he was led up to the matter of calculating latitude by a highly qualified naval officer with the question:— ''Now skipper; when you are out on the Dogger Bank, what is the most important thing you must know?''

''How to bloody well catch fish, of course,'' Harry answered — And they failed him!

Australian mate Bill Nance, painting overside in the *Cambria*. After serving a year in *Cambria* he sailed home to Australia in the 27 foot *Cardinal Vertue*, single handed, via the Cape of Good Hope, returning later round Cape Horn.

The *Quartette*.

CHAPTER FIVE

To Sail the Broad Ocean

NEVER a book worm and hating mathematics from my early school days, I entered the London School of Navigation like a doomed man going to the scaffold. I was sure I would never pass the Board of Trade Examinations. I stared at the volumes and columns of figures, the log sines, cosines and haversines, the meridional parts, logarithms, hour angles and azimuths until my head felt like a football and my eyes were sore and red. Sometimes I would get one or two problems rights, more often, none at all. And my exercise books were thick with the instructor's red marks. He was a Nova Scotiaman, patient and humorous. But when he wrote in the margin:

> "Remember you are increasing your west longitude. According to this you are going stern first into Central Russia"

— I went out to the pub intending to quit the Navigation School, and bumped into an old seafaring friend named Peter Erikson, a Cockney-Norwegian whose adventures ashore and afloat would fill a book.

> "There's a man looking for you. Wants to take a Ramsgate trawler across the Western Ocean. You're just the chap. Here's his address. I can't go. I'm too old. I'm long ways over eighty and I'm only hanging on to wear these clothes out. I can drink beer and tell a yarn — den fall down dead and der people vill say 'silly old bastard, serve him right.' Dat is how seamen die if dey don't drown first."

In his heyday that was often the case.

Erikson departed for Greenwich, where he lived aboard an old barge. I to the London suburb of Lewisham to find the man who wanted to sail westward in a Ramsgate trawler.

I found him in his lodgings and he proved to be a schoolmaster named Sinclair. He had had no sea-training other than buying two yachts and wrecking them both. He was a small, wiry little man approaching sixty years of age. He had been told of a sailing trawler for sale at Ramsgate for £110, similar to one he had bought some years earlier as a yacht and piled up on the sea-wall at Westkappel in Holland. He had first been taught how to sail a little boat at the age of 30 by a fellow schoolmaster who was one of the seafaring Rigdens of Whitstable. Anyone named Rigden in Whitstable was sure to be some sort of a sailor or smacksman. At one time they populated half the town, the other half being occupied by the numerous family of Perkins, who were nearly all shipwrights and boat-builders. There was a smaller enclave of Strood (or Stroud) who were seamen born and bred. Two of them, in turn, sailed as mate in the King's beautiful *Britannia* and knew the days of the mighty spars and jackyard topsails — when seamen were gentlemen and gentlemen were seamen.

A day was appointed when Sinclair and I could travel to Ramsgate and inspect the vessel he had heard about. She was named the *Quartette* and had been built at Galmpton in Devon in 1896. She had not always been in the Ramsgate fleet and had at one time fished out of Lowestoft, during which period one of my relatives from Kessingland nearby had served in her and was a great admirer of her easy motion in bad weather.

On the way to Ramsgate we collected Charlie Perkins from Whitstable to act as our professional surveyor. As his only surveying instrument he brought a heavy hammer, saying "If she don't ring right I'll soon know there's something wrong with her."

We found the *Quartette* berthed against a wall where she would dry out and as the tide left her we could walk round in comfort. Charlie periodically belaboured her with his hammer, so lustily that if there had been any soft spots, the hammer would have gone right through her. But she "rung like a bell." Sinclair and I poked about inside but the only defects we found were minor ones and easily repairable. Her running and standing rigging was in bad shape but she had two good mainsails and plenty of sound canvas in the way of jibs, topsails and foresails.

She was skippered by a man named Fairbrass, and, good as his name, his price was fair enough — £110. We bought her.

I was sorry in a way to have been instrumental in the old fellow giving her up because she was the very last fishing boat to work out of Ramsgate harbour under sail alone — the last survivor of the once magnificent fleet about which the old greybeards loved to tell their ever-vivid tales, recollecting incidents and passages of fifty years ago as though they were but yesterday. But I suppose he would have sold her anyway and I must confess that I was so taken by the beauty of her lines and her obvious ability to ride any weather that all thoughts of having any other boat for an ocean cruise were immediately driven from my mind. If I could have a share of her with Sinclair I was content. I would never have a chance on my own account of sailing such a lovely vessel.

Charlie Perkins agreed to haul the *Quartette* out on his slipway at Whitstable, where the boatyard opened directly on to the bleak shingle beach. There he would strip her out, re-rig and re-fit her and have shipwrights sheath her bottom with muntz metal as a protection against tropical teredo worm. This muntz metal (incorrectly called "brass" by local fishermen) was frequently used to sheath the old Whitstable smacks and the shipyard hands were accustomed to working with it. Actually it is an alloy of copper and zinc and is thus suitable for use on iron fastened vessels. Whereas pure copper sheathing sets up a murderous galvanic action on iron fastenings, this muntz metal seems to have little effect. Smacks thus sheathed for many years and eventually broken up through old age were shown to me by Charlie Perkins and it was obvious that the effect on the fastenings had been almost negligible.

The method of putting on the metal looks simple enough but in practice requires the craftsmanship and skill of the professional shipwright. It is no job for the amateur or even the "chap handy with his tools." The bottom fastenings are first examined and any doubtful ones renewed or doubled. Then the caulking irons are fetched out and every seam hardened or re-done. The next operation is to give the bottom a thick and sticky coat of tar, on which is stuck a layer of horse hair. Old fashioned shipwrights call this the "hair and blare", over which goes a lining of ship's felt, on top of all this go the sheets of muntz metal. Once the vessel "settles down" after launching she is not likely to worry you much in the way of pumping.

The business of purchase complete, Sinclair and I hustled off down to Ramsgate again to fetch the *Quartette* to Whitstable. We found on board, looking after her, a little old man named Harry Solly who had been mate of her for so many years that he almost seemed to be part and parcel of the vessel. Sinclair, as was natural for a man with an academic training, tended to regard him as a scruffy little bundle of ignorance, but the worthy Harry was not such a

A view of the *Quartette*'s deck.

Sinclair on the *Quartette*'s deck.

fool as he seemed. He had not fished the North Sea under sail all his life and learned nothing. From him I learned a great deal about the *Quartette* and her gear which stood me in good stead months afterwards when there were repairs to do aloft in mid-ocean.

He told me he used to fish with seven men aboard but when the steam capstan was put in the crew were reduced to three. ''But that capstan don't mend tore nets or go aloft to clear a foul topsail'', he commented. However, he had learned to take great care of this steam capstan, the boiler for which was housed just forward of the cabin. He showed us how to use it for every possible purpose on board — warping out of the basin, heaving the anchor up, setting the sails, hauling the small boat aboard and even for setting up the shroud lanyards. If there was work to be done Harry never failed to have a head of steam ready.

We took him on to help us sail round to the East Swale, where we were to await suitable tides and weather for Charlie Perkins to haul her out. I liked Harry's uncanny judgement as he luffed her out of the harbour with the tide running swiftly across the pier heads, after which Sinclair and I took turns at the tiller to get the feel of her. She was certainly a nice hull to handle; no flyer, but sure and easy. Just what we wanted.

After we had hauled round the North Foreland and met a moderate westerly breeze above Margate roads, we found it necessary to bring up in the Gore Channel as the night ebb came away. Jib and foresail were taken in as we came to the wind and once the anchor was down I moved to the throat and peak halliards with the intention of lowering the mainsail. Harry was horrified.

"We never lower that" he said "till we get back home. Reef it perhaps but never lower it. Might not get it up again if it comes on bad weather."

There was a lot of good sense in what he said. It was no task for a couple of weaklings to get that gaff and heavy canvas aloft and properly set. So we took his advice and laid at anchor all that ebb with the mainsail set, pushing the smack up over her chain so that it led tight down under her bow. I was wondering how we were going to heave it up with all that strain on it but Harry, sensing what was in my mind as I looked over the stemhead, winked and jerked his thumb towards the steam capstan. "That'll pull he out" he said. Of course, I had forgotten about this fearsome thing the old ship secreted in her bowels. And sure enough, on the slack water, to the accompaniment of a hiss and rattle, the fifteen fathoms of chain came in with hardly any physical effort on our part. Off we went "over the land" to the West Last buoy, Columbine, Pollard Spit and the Swale, eventually letting go off Harty Ferry.

From there Harry said goodbye to his old ship, not without some regret I thought, as he gave a quick backward glance when I put him ashore in the boat. Hard as nails, an undemonstrative little chap, I knew he was leaving a life he had known since boyhood to end his days in an atmosphere of uncertainty and unfamiliarity which is the lot of many an ageing seaman.

Soon the day came for hauling out and the shipyard sent young Harold Strood to act as our pilot to the slipway. Marks had been set up to help in possitioning the vessel as she arrived off the beach. Harold acted as bosun and rigger on the yard in the winter but during the summer months went racing in big yachts, being at this time mate of the King's *Britannia*. He was a natural, born sailor, and was just as much at home steering a fishing smack as a smart yacht. He sailed her in so that she stopped dead in line with the slipway and the yard had a direct and easy pull to haul her up with the aid of a wire and winch which had been got ready on shore. Now at last I felt that the trade winds were getting nearer and as Sinclair and I walked round her the next day we agreed that in the *Quartette* we had got a ship fit to go anywhere.

So, away I went back to Navigation School and also to try to earn enough money for my share of the fitting out. The new standing and running rigging I could make myself, for I was no stranger to that sort of work, but the sheathing and shipwright work was likely to run up to something near £150. While Sinclair settled down to live aboard I rode a bike to London and set about making a complete new set of wire rigging for a 50 foot motor yacht in the Albert Dock. This was a well paid job and good practice for the *Quartette* rig out; and before long I obtained another week's wiresplicing work aboard a yacht at Chiswick. In the evenings and week-ends I wrote articles and reports for newspapers and magazines and acted as relief nightwatchman on a road repair job at Lee. All this brought in a steady stream of wealth until I reckoned I had enough to pay my half share of the *Quartette*'s fit out. Being very taken up with the idea of sailing in her I did not reveal to anyone, not even to Sinclair, my temporary methods of acquiring sterling for fear he would consider me too rough a diamond to partner him in a highly respectable yachting enterprise.

So I hauled out my bike again and rode the 50 miles back down to Whitstable (the train fare was worth a coil of rope) with the intention of setting about making the new standing rigging for the *Quartette*.

I got a surprise when I reached there for preparations had gone far beyond what I had anticipated. Harold Strood had already made nearly all the rigging and professional hands had been employed to do nearly all the jobs I had thought I could tackle without a great deal of expense. Seeing my dismay and sensing some resentment on my part, Sinclair said he had ordered these things to be done entirely off his own bat with the object of getting the ship ready in the shortest possible time and was quite willing to foot the bill himself. In this way he was over-generous and actuated by the best motive — to get the ship under way as soon as possible — but the soaring shipyard bill left me with a feeling of indebtedness which I could never pay off. The final figure was £537, towards which my hardearned £75 looked a bit silly. But Sinclair would only accept £50 of it and said that he would reckon the bill cheap if he got in a year or two of good deep water cruising in such a fine vessel.

It was a winter fit-out, often held up by bad weather because practically all the work on the smack was being done out in the open. But even on wet days there was always something to get on with, such as clearing out all the "ironstone" ballast and replacing it with cleaned and tarred pig iron so that the shipwrights could lower the floor of the hold. This was to be used as a general store for sails, rope and food. Racks were built each side for the spare canvas. The forecastle was re constructed with two roomy bunks and locker space for the use of our anticipated crew. Sinclair and I were to sleep aft in the old cabin, where there was five feet of headroom.

Dramatic tales of our proposed voyage soon spread along the foreshore and although the most frequent was that "she's the boat what's going to set off round the world," I did hear through various channels that we were going to search for treasure in the Pacific, take an expedition to the Antarctic or (oh, dark secret!) engage in some nefarious smuggling venture for which mysterious alterations were being carried out below decks at night (probably Sinclair and me cleaning the lockers out by lamplight.)

Almost every day old fishermen and sailormen came round to see how we were getting on. Whitstable is the home port of many an old sea-dog and it is sometimes worth a guinea a minute to hear them talk. Without any attempt at boastfulness or exaggeration, they yarned of their days on the Dogger Bank, in the sailing colliers (schooners, brigs, brigantines, ketches and billy-boys) which used to bring the coal from the north up to London — 200 of them belonged to Whitstable — and of an occasional deep sea voyage by way of a change to

Australia and the West Indies. Nearly all of them had started their seafaring careers by serving in the Whitstable smacks — trawling, oyster dredging, shrimping, five-fingering and occasionally running across to Flushing with mussels. Although these smacks are cutter rigged they are known locally as "yawls", which is probably a derivation from the old Norse word "yole" still used in the Shetlands. One of the smacks used in this latter trade had been built by Charlie Perkins and his brother Dick after the breakup of the old Whitstable Shipping Company's Yard, where they were joint foremen. She was named *Stormy Petrel* and (to skip a few years) she eventually came into my ownership for fishing off the Essex and Suffolk coasts.

One of these hardy old stalwarts was George Paysden, bent almost double by some dreadful operation, but mentally vigorous as he had been thirty years before. His bright blue eyes were as keen as ever and as far as I could tell he gave not a thought to his infirmity nor required sympathy or help. He had sailed in both square and fore and aft rigs — "everything except a spritty barge" — on the coast, fishing and deep sea.

"Skippers of ships and barques" he told us one day "used to like to get us young fellers from the smacks and coasters because we were a bit smarter than some of the packet rats they got out of the lodging houses."

George did not describe places he had been to abroad by their character or attractions on shore but always from the seaman's point of view. This place would be a good anchorage with a mud bottom and safe in any weather; another a bad berth "where we always kept our topsails loosed"; another always hot and dry and "a good place to get our sails mended". Whatever colourful scenes there were on shore they did not mean a thing to George. His business was to

View of *Quartette*'s deck from the masthead.

33

Quartette on Perkins' slipway at Whitstable. Full-bodied,
sea-kindly lines.

make a successful voyage, look after his ship and cargo, and get back home to Whitstable.

In the evenings Sinclair and I used to take a walk up to his cottage and yarn about the sea and ships over a cup of coffee. His wife knew what it was to be a sailor's wife and she told us that she always packed George's bag for him when he **went** off to sea, knowing every item he would want for the particular voyage he **was** going on. George said he never looked into his bag until he got aboard and not once in all his seafaring career did he find anything missing. But there was one occasion when she refused to pack his bag. George had been sent for to go north and join a topsail schooner lying there loaded with coal for London. The mate had been taken ill and the skipper had particularly asked the Whitstable owners for George to be sent to him.

Mrs. Paysden said "Something told me that if George joined that ship I should never see him again. I begged him not to go but he called me a fool and told me to get his bag ready. 'I'm not packing your bag to join that ship, George' I told him and he got real angry with me and started ramping round the house and getting his things together himself. Then he calmed down and I went on my knees and said 'Please don't go'. In the end, he threw his bag down and said 'All right, woman. If you say so, I won't go. Women see things us men don't, though Lord knows what I shall tell the skipper when I see him'."

George never saw that skipper again. The schooner was overtaken by a midwinter blizzard just as she was entering the West Swin channel. In a blinding snowstorm she drove on to the Maplins and was lost with all hands.

George nodded as she finished her tale. "That was the hand of Providence" he said.

The wealth of maritime knowledge to be gleaned at Whitstable did not come only from old sea dogs but also from the shipwrights themselves, who still used the ancient methods of their forebears. It was a pleasure to watch them use their tools and there did not seem to be a single job of work connected with boats and ships which they could not tackle with an expert knowledge.

Nothing was done hurriedly, nothing was skimped. I remember watching one old man named Rigden who was entrusted with the task of re-fastening the bottom before the metal sheathing went on. He seemed to work very, very slowly. Every fastening was regarded thoughtfully for as much as two or three minutes before it was driven home and then examined with great care after the deft blows of his hammer had made it a permanent part of the *Quartette*. I think that perhaps Sinclair's words described him best.

"When I first saw him work, my heart sank. I thought he was so slow that he would never finish the job. But I was amazed at the end of the day to see how much work the old fellow had got through."

It was while we were at Whitstable that I got a satisfactory answer to a question I had asked shipwrights before, both in England and abroad. "Why does a wooden vessel generally need more repairs done on the port side than on the starboard side?" This was always an accepted fact in the old shipyards and when a vessel was up for repair a knowing shipwright who did not want a lot of work would always take the starboard side if he got the chance. American and Canadian shipwrights have told me the same without ever being able to explain the reason why.

So I asked Charlie Perkins. Taciturn and thoughtful, like all his breed, he looked at me steadily for several seconds with those clear blue eyes of his, as if to make sure I was serious, and then transferred his gaze to the pebbles. Presently he said; "That's right, what you say. The starboard side is always the best." And then he passed on. I thought I had drawn a blank but then four days later when I was burning rust off our anchor shackle with a bonfire of shavings he came up behind me and tapped my shoulder.

"I've been thinking over what you asked me about the starboard side being better than the port; and I'll tell you why it is. When we used to build a vessel the master-shipwright always worked on the starboard side (same as a skipper always lived on the starboard side). The best hand available used to take charge of the port side and they used to pick teams before they started. The master had first pick as it was a feather in the cap of the shipwright who was the master's first choice. So, having first pick, the master always got the best men, who worked with him on the starboard side."

"Now the timber would always be stacked close handy and the master and his team, being able to work that little bit faster than the others, were always going to the stack first and picking out the best of the timber. Naturally they would not take any knotty or badly cut pieces and these fell to the lot of the slower team working on the port side. That's why the starboard side lasts better. Same with your *Quartette*. Better timber and better work done."

And for a well thought out solution to an old mystery I think that explanation of Charlie's takes some beating.

The 27 foot cutter *Thelma* in which the author and a friend sailed from London to the Pacific.

CHAPTER SIX

A Memorable Launch

THE day the *Quartette* was launched off Whitstable beach is still remembered, with some degree of hilarity, by the shipwrights and seamen who witnessed or took part in the great event.

For a fortnight she had stood there, the major fit-out finished, running rigging rove and sails bent, looking almost like a new ship with her sleek grey painted sides and shining spars. Her topsides had been "dubbed down" with adzes to remove the thick coating of tar so that we could paint her a light colour to resist the heat of the tropical sun. The rigging I was not very happy about because it had been put on trawler fashion, which did not allow for the almost unbelievable chafe set up by ocean rollers, light winds or a week or two in the doldrums. This I knew from past experience in the cutter *Thelma*, the Yankee schooner *Franklin Barnett* and from meetings with other ocean wayfarers in small boats. The many hours I spent aloft at sea in the months to follow, altering, repairing and replacing both running and standing rigging did not help me to swallow my resentment at Sinclair's innocent running up of a big shipyard bill for all this work.

The spring tides on which it was Charlie's intention to launch the *Quartette* were below their predicted level and also accompanied by onshore winds; so he would not risk sending her down the slipway. By the time the feeble neaps had in their turn timidly damped the foreshore there was a change in the weather and on the next big tide there came a gentle southerly breeze from off the town.

Charlie stood at the top of the slipway watching the tide rise towards the marks he had made on the baulks. Occasionally he glanced up at the sky. All his yard hands were round at the harbour doing urgent repairs to a sailing barge. Presently he called young "Stormy" Strood, the apprentice lad, who was wearily bagging up shavings round the saw bench.

"Nip round to the harbour and tell all hands to come to the yard. We'll launch the *Quartette* this tide."

There were six of them all told and Harold Strood once more boarded us as pilot and bosun-in-charge of lines and moorings. He had laid a mooring off the beach and a small line was run off to this so that as soon as the vessel was well afloat (being launched stern first) we could haul her head to seaward and get her under way.

Quartette ready to launch.

As she became waterborne all six hands clambered aboard to help us get clear of the beach but just as we got her head round a black cloud came sweeping out of the north west — an onshore squall.

For a few moments the *Quartette* was in grave danger. We were hardly clear of the ends of the slipway and the beach groynes were to leeward. Only a thin cotton line held us off the beach.

Hastily we cast off the mainsail gaskets. Harold Strood rushed to the tiller.

"Up with them bloody sails" he bawled at the yard hands. "Up with 'em. Quick."

The heavy mainsail went up as though it only weighed a few ounces, three strong men on each halyard. I had already got a No. 2 jib ready on the bowsprit and the squall swept down upon us just as we cast away on the port tack.

Harold was at the helm and he looked grim and anxious as the *Quartette* sagged to leeward before picking up enough way to start griping to windward. The beach seemed very close. I wondered if she would hit. But Harold was on his own ground. He needed no leadline even if there had been time to use one. He knew every hump and stone of the offshore flats. When close to the edge of the groyne which had some ugly looking stakes sticking out of the water he sung out "Lee-oh".

As we surged past the end of the slipway again we caught a glimpse of Charlie Perkins, alone on shore, waving and shouting.

"He wants you to put us ashore" said one of the shipwrights. "We're wanted on that barge job."

Harold gave a grim smile.

"Not a hope" he replied. "We're not clear yet. Looks bad to windward."

To and fro we tacked, gaining very little against the on-shore set and drift, Harold watching his marks as he steered by crouching low and peering under the boom. Like a true seaman, he had confidence in his own skill and judgement to get the *Quartette* out of a dangerous situation. Any crazy fool might blow across an ocean in a small boat but in a predicament such as we were in, then one can see who is the real seaman and who is not. And if Harold Strood had not been aboard that day the cruise of the *Quartette* might have ended in disaster on Whitstable beach.

We made seven tacks before he straightened his back and gave a sigh of obvious relief.

"She's coming off lovely now" he said. "Get the mizzen on her, Bob".

"What about the shipwrights?" I asked.

"Well" said Harold, "It's too far now to get them back to the yard. They'll have to come with us up the Swale and get back from there."

The shipwrights seemed rather to enjoy the situation. It was quite an adventure for them to be shanghaied off to sea like this and they vied with each other about the tales they would have to tell when they got back home.

"Charlie'll be something savage" chuckled the oldest one. "There he stands with all the yard to hisself and all his hands gone away to sea."

By the time we had rounded the Pollard Spit into the East Swale river the wind was coming out south west again and the ebb was away. Abreast of a prominent house named *The Sportsman* at Seasalter we had to anchor; and now came the pantomime of landing the six shipwrights on the mudflats to stumble and slither their way to the firm ground. I shall never forget the sight of this gallant little band of cheerful souls, plastered with mud, some occasionally sinking knee deep into slimy potholes, making their wet weary way to the seawall, their gaze (and their minds) fixed unflinchingly on the door of *The Sportsman*. Where I learned later, they "made a day of it" with many a thrilling tale of their voyage in the *Quartette* which grew to a hair raising episode by the time they had dried their clothes and expressed a pained surprise at the landlord's insistence four hours later that the law required him to close his premises.

Harold, his day's work done, remained on board for the night and on the morning tide sailed with us up to the anchorage at Harty Ferry, where Sinclair and I could straighten things out and get ready for a trial trip in the estuary.

We had let it be known that we required two hands for an ocean cruise who would be willing to share in the running expenses of the ship and we eventually put an advertisement in a yachting magazine. We got the usual spate of stupid replies from the sort of people who would obviously be hopeless and useless, but there were two very promising customers, by the tone of their letters — one from

West Mersea and one from Falmouth. West Mersea being fairly close at hand, we suggested that the writer should come to see the *Quartette*, and there arrived one day a lanky, quiet spoken young man of 22 years of age who said his name was John Bell. He modestly admitted to some knowledge of boat sailing and was useful with carpentry tools. I took a liking to him immediately and in the end Sinclair and I agreed to sail the *Quartette* to West Mersea and pick him up there.

The letter from Falmouth was signed Henry Trefusis (as Cornish a name as one could ever wish to hear) and he arranged to come and see us in London, for it was our intention to lay in stores in one of the P.L.A.* docks.

The trip to West Mersea started badly. On a fine day, with a southerly breeze, we sailed out round the Columbine and as she idled her way out to the Four Fathom Channel I went aloft to alter the lead of the peak halyard, mouse some hook blocks and splice a jackstay for the topsail. While thus engaged I felt a jerk as I sat on the mainmast head and thought at first it was due to the rigging having stretched as she rolled slightly in the gentle swell. Presently I got another, more decisive jerk and I looked down at Sinclair standing unconcernedly at the tiller. A quick glance round and I saw that we were inside the few buoys that mark this narrow channel and sung out "We're touching the Spaniard."

Sinclair sprang to life immediately and shoved the helm hard down, but he was too late. We were on and the ebb was well away. Slowly, as the water left her, the *Quartette* settled gently on her side. A pretty picture we must have looked, stuck up there on the highest part of the Middle Spaniard sand, bound across the world and not even out of sight of Whitstable.

Fortunately the weather remained calm and that evening we floated off again. Next day we joined a fleet of barges going down the West Swin and, crossing the Spitway, turned to windward up the Blackwater as the breeze freshened from the southwest.

It was almost dark when we arrived off Mersea Quarters and Sinclair, who so wanted to be Captain, stood her inshore while I stowed the topsail and mizzen. A few minutes later he had put us hard and fast on the Nass shoal, close to the beacon. Fortunately it was flood tide but there was a fresh wind and a tidy popple. We let go the main anchor and she bounced clear of it so that we could give her some chain and, after a couple of very uncomfortable hours, dropped off into deep water.

Next day we rowed up to Mersea Hard, met John Bell, old Bill Wyatt (the "Admiral of Mersea"), my artist friend Archie White, the Finnish skipper of the barque *Alastor* which laid in the Blackwater, and several other seafaring and yachting aquaintances.

John Bell could not sail with us right away so Sinclair and I took the *Quartette* up London River, eventually to moor in the East India Dock to make our final preparations.

*P.L.A. = Port of London Authority

There the Cornishman, Henry Trefusis, paid us a visit and once more we seemed to have had the good fortune to bump into just the sort of chap we wanted. Pleasant and cheerful, he had, like so many Cornishmen, a natural trait for the sea and had been brought up "with a tiller in his hand" as the fishermen say. Although educated at a University he confessed that he was more interested in boats than in scholastic studies and had at one time served before the mast in the old barquentine *Waterwitch*, in which I also had spent some of my boyhood days. So we had much in common. He agreed to join us at Falmouth, which we intended to make our last port of call in England.

Thus, with the crew settled, we set about taking in stores of every description. At my suggestion, having been too hungry at sea in the past to forget it, we took a large stock of dried beans and peas, which, for the sake of simplicity, we stowed in brand new dustbins. With the exception of a large stock of corned beef, we cut down on tinned food as we had both found in previous cruises that this is an unsatisfactory and expensive way of storing a ship. Later we took on big stocks of potatoes, onions and any sort of vegetable or fruit which could be preserved for any length of time.

Well wishers came by the dozen and presented us with all sorts of odds and ends ranging from a Primus oven to a small library.

When we were in the East India Dock there were times when I began to think the voyage of the *Quartette* would never start. Friends came and friends went — and more friends came. Delays and farewell pints kept putting back the day of departure from one week to the next until some six months had passed since the time we went down to Ramsgate on the train to purchase the trawler. But at last all was ready and all our dustbins and cases were full of flour, beans, peas, corned beef, oatmeal, salt horse, hard biscuits and such like — enough to last four hungry seamen six months at a pinch. Our water supply of 250 gallons

John Bell prepares dinner on deck while the ship steers herself on a tiller line.

41

Henry Trefusis gives us a tune in the Dog Watch.

was topped up and even iron rations in sealed tins were put by in case of emergency.

While alongside the quay we were in distinguished company, the famous Antarctic exploration ship *Discovery* lay close by, an immensely strong though not very handsome steam barque which had carried Shackleton's first expedition. I found an old friend aboard there acting as watchman — the ship's sailmaker, Joe Palmer. He told me much of the expedition and her personnel from his own point of view which I am sure would not be published officially in any account of the enterprise; and certainly I would not repeat it for fear of libel. But he was an old sea-dog and a first class man at his job and what he thought of what he called ''Navy sailors'' aboard a sailing vessel would have taken the paint off the bulwarks. But beneath all his predjudices and grumblings was a dogged faith in Shackleton himself and an overriding wish that his old commander could come to life and take the old *Discovery* to sea again.

From Joe I acquired a small black kitten, one of many which the *Discovery*'s cat had produced since the old ship had been laid up in the dock, and this tiny creature I established aboard the *Quartette* complete with sand-box, milk supply, special cat food and even a packet of vitamin pills which a doctor friend said he would need on a long voyage. We called him Disco, after his birth-ship.

At last we towed out of the dock and it was a great tonic to me to get the canvas on her and feel her heel to the breeze as we went away down the estuary. Various friends accompanied us down the Channel as we intended to call at Poole and Falmouth, our Cornish sailor, Henry Trefusis, having arranged to join us at the latter port. John Bell came along but was unwell for most of the westward trip owing to the severe effect of a recent vaccination; so he had no chance to show his mettle when we ran into a tidy breeze from the south west when we were off Start Point.

It was one of those breezes which has put an end there to more than one ambitious cruise — a regular channel buster with slashing rain and a breaking sea so that the water ran down your neck and up through your socks and you felt as though your under pants were held up by a wet eel round your waist. But it was a good shake down and at least one major weakness was discovered and which we had not reckoned with.

Mizzen masts in ketches are always hard to stay forward and as I was tucking a reef into this sail one night I noticed the mast take a threatening lurch aft. I thought at first that in rigging out we had not hove the fore shroud tight enough, for it is usual to cant the mast well forward. But as I stood on the taffrail the boom fell with a thump on my toes. It was very dark and it being obvious that something serious was wrong I hastily lowered the sail. Archie White was at the tiller at the time and Sinclair off watch asleep in his bunk.

As I looked aloft while the sail was coming down I could see the mizzen mast waving drunkenly against the sky, and down by the mast coat the deck planks looked like being ripped out as the spar swayed further aft.

I dashed down below, woke Sinclair and unshipped the cabin table so that I could get at the mizzen mast step in the counter. There was the oak mast step lying on the floor and the heel of the mast was waving about, smashing out panelling and ready to lever anything within range to destruction.

A couple of big wedges steadied it temporarily while we rigged a forward tackle on deck and this gave us time to get a chain lashing round the heel before it could do any more damage. This meant that as soon as we could get into Falmouth the mast would have to be lifted and a new step fastened in.

Next day we sailed into the harbour and no sooner was the anchor down than a small sailing boat shot alongside and over the rail sprang Henry Trefusis — which I thought was a right, proper and traditional way for a Cornishman to join a ship.

At Falmouth the last of our well wishers departed with many a merry pint and tot and we set about putting our wayward mizzen mast to rights. From Penryn we borrowed two long fir poles which I rigged up as sheer legs and thus lifted the mizzen high enough for a local shipwright to put in a new step, the old one having split at the fastenings. This done, we were ready to say goodbye to old England — we did not know for how long — and John Bell and Henry Trefusis stowed their gear in our newly built forecastle.

It was May, and better weather we could not have wished for. With the wind in the north we set the lot and soon Henry had waved his last farewell to the shore — for he was a native here and heir to lands as well. In the dog watches we sat round the quarter and yarned, getting to know each other better than if we had met on shore a score of times. We talked of everything from seagulls to navigation and finished up with a long discussion on ship's lavatories. This was by no means an unfruitful subject as it has always been, and still is, a major problem in most sailing vessels.

I was once skipper of an old schooner in the coal trade which had so small a lavatory in her little teak wheelhouse that it was impossible to get out of it when it was to windward. (To leeward it was a job to stay in it!) The flushing arrangements were very simple, depending upon gravity, being a hole down through the counter. But the interesting part of this affair was that when to windward there was provided what was known as a ''hauling off warp''. This venerable piece of hemp must have been there almost since the ship was built in 1876 for in it there were all manner of old seamen's knots and sennets, some of which I have never seen in these times. Perhaps each user vied with his predecessor, but in spite of its humble use I always regarded this couple of fathom as an item of interest. It was my intention to take it home with me but an Irishman chopped it off one night as we lay in Waterford and, as it transpired, sold it to a wealthy gentleman. If that gentleman now has it hanging in his hall, as I believe he has, I hope he may chance to read these few lines and thus be informed what it was used for.

John and Henry told us of the marvellous contraptions installed in up-to-date yachts but, like most yachtsmen, felt uneasy about having holes in the side of the boat below the water line and also about the possibility of someone forgetting to close the valve. Sinclair's idea of a bucket in gimbals seemed as good as any but the first watch (8 o'clock) brought an end to this very informative talk.

We divided into two watches — Sinclair and Henry in one and John and myself in the other. Each pair stood the customary four hours watch dividing the steering into a couple of hours each. If the weather was fine and all well the man not at the tiller could go below and turn in but was liable to be called out if required.

By this system, we nearly always got six hours sleep off the reel — four while the other watch was on duty and two while your partner took the helm. It worked satisfactorily and we stuck to it.

We had decided to waste no time on the Spanish coast — or on Spanish beauties — and make straight for Madeira. Sinclair and I each worked out our navigation sights independently and by different methods — I don't think he really approved of mine — but they always worked out to practically the same position.

Biscay was kind to us. We rolled away westward and at times did not have enough wind to hold the main boom out. Our noon to noon progress was little over the 70 miles mark and on one day we found that the inset into the Bay over a 24 hour period was as much as 26 miles. It was this inset which used to cause so much anxiety to the captains of square rigged ships and they always used to get out to ten degrees west longtitude before daring to bear up and head south to pick up the north east trades.

At times the wind was dead fair and we hitched out the light reaching foresail as a spinnaker on a long boathook. In these paltry winds and Atlantic swell I could see that our heavy trawler sails were not going to be exactly ideal for tropical airs later on.

One of the mistakes often made by intending ocean cruisers is to fit out with mighty strong flax sails and heavy gear as though they were going to ride out or run before all the storms and hurricanes the Lord ever sent. But in actual practice most of an ocean cruiser's sailing is done in fine weather, light tropical breezes or steady and pleasant trade winds. No vessel is doing much good with the gear slatting and banging about like all hell let loose.

At first we rigged a lee boom tackle from the after end of the spar round to the bow but this was not very successful as it was impossible to keep it bar tight or to prevent the up and down movement. Eventually I went aloft and rigged a rolling vang on the gaff end in spritty barge fashion and led this down to the anchor windlass. This kept the spars quiet (funny how these ancient ideas work out best) but nothing would stop the heavy loose footed sail from performing an operation something like a housewife shaking a mat.

Before long "Tom Fool's Earring" at the clew showed signs of chafing through so I rove a piece of chain in its place and lashed the cringle snug down to the boom. Next day, looking aloft as the sun came up I saw that our peak halliard had chafed through and just as I called John to come and take the helm while I went aloft the rope parted and left the gaff suspended only by the topsail sheet.

Hastily I clambered up on to the gaff and re-rove the long end which had fallen through the block, and knotted the two broken ends together so that we could take the weight on them. If the topsail sheet had parted and let the peak fall with a clatter we might have had a nasty accident, apart from damaging the

"All Fast". Disco the cat never knew shore life. Born aboard *Discovery*, he joined the *Quartette* and died at sea. He was given a sailor's burial off the mouth of the Amazon.

The author and Disco aboard *Quartette*.

topsail. But it held on and John and Henry hoisted away on the knotted halliard while I parcelled it with canvas as a precaution against the same thing happening again.

I now set about showing them how to make chafing gear — which is simple enough anyway — and each man spent an hour every afternoon making long lengths of lamb's tails and wrinkle for future use. It was obvious we were going to need a good stock of it.

This reminds me of a peculiar word I have often read in yachting books and magazines, where chafing gear has been referred to as "baggy wrinkle". I feel sure that whoever invented or heard of this expression got hold of the wrong end of the stick when listening to some ancient mariner whose accent was perhaps a bit thicker or richer than could be readily understood by an educated townsman. When I first went to sea in barquentines and schooners we always had kept in the half deck or bosun's locker a *bag of wrinkle*, which was a sack containing all the odd ends cut off from splices, useless short bits of rope, or any unlaid strands left over from grommets and suchlike. When all other work was done and we were not quite dead or asleep on our feet, the mate would bring out this blasted *bag of wrinkle* and set us to cutting it up in even lengths and working it into and round pieces of point line or three stranded spunyarn stretched along the deck. The result was called chafing gear; and it was all made from the *bag of wrinkle*.

"Baggy Wrinkle" my foot!

John and Henry could soon make chafing gear with their eyes shut and within a few days we had a good stock of it stowed away for future use. While we were thus busy with doldrums drill we picked up the Portuguese trades, a steady northerly wind which blows most of the year south of Cape Finnisterre. They are a sort of introduction to the North East Trades further south and are lovely to run with in a south bound vessel. It was as comfortable aboard the *Quartette* with her wonderfully easy sea-motion as for Grandma in her rocking chair. And warmer, too.

Our daily runs now began to get us somewhere. From the creeping seventies we bowled into the one hundred and fifties. Once she ran 169. No wonder the Portuguese were among the early navigators to America. They had such lovely weather and fair winds to start with. They didn't have to bash to windward out of the English Channel and hazard the gales of the Bay of Biscay like their English rivals. And no wonder the mariners of England were of a hardier breed.

After a few days these winds petered out to a calm and we took the opportunity to lower the mainsail and reeve a new peak halliard, also shipping a new topping lift shackle which had opened out in the slatting about. I seemed to be spending all my spare time aloft.

While we lay becalmed a small whale came round us and we tried to devise means of catching him but had no gear heavy enough for such an operation. Even if we had had a harpoon big enough and a rope long enough we all pictured the *Quartette* whizzing off in the wrong direction and finishing up as an Antarctic expedition. So John fetched out a very antiquated pistol which looked as though it had not been fired for many a grandfather's birthday; but courageously he loaded it with shot and we all stood clear. The thing went off rather earlier than anticipated with the result that a number of holes appeared in the peak of the mizzen. John agreed with us that it would be best to put the pistol away and he never used it again. If whales are capable of an ironic smile that whale must have had one on his face as he leisurely swam away.

We had been at sea a fortnight by the time we approached Madeira, and as we closed to within fifty miles of where we reckoned it was the winds fell light and variable, as so often happens when there is an isolated bit of land stuck in a wide ocean. To my mind this helped to confirm our position, but we took a few more sights and then steered a diagonal course to pick up the mountain right on the bowsprit end. Both Sinclair and I felt rather cocky about this as we had been bold enough to trust our longitude working rather than work well to the eastward and run the latitude down, which is a much easier way of making an island landfall. But some credit is due to Henry as well for the day before we saw the land he commented, with a true Cornishman's inhibition: "By the break in the sky to the southwest and the colour of the water, and this change of wind and the smell of manure, I'll bet a pound to a pinch of snuff we'll see land tomorrow". And we did.

We were exactly fifteen and a half days out from Falmouth and the distance about sixteen hundred miles.

CHAPTER SEVEN

To Lonely Ocean Isles

SINCLAIR was no stranger to Funchal, the port and capital of the island, and he took the helm as we approached the anchorage off the town. But no sooner had we let go and stowed our sails than a burly figure in a motor boat ranged alongside and hailed us with a voice like a friendly fog-horn. It was Coelho, a great, husky Portuguese chap with bright blue eyes and a ginger moustache. He had served in square rig and was now "runner" for the local shipping agents. He knew Sinclair from when he had sailed there in the yacht *Joan*. Being a good friend and a man of some influence he soon had us berthed alongside a jetty in a corner of the bay where we could walk ashore in comfort. He was a great friend to us, this Coelho, and even more so when he found that his boss had been a friend of Henry Trefusis at Oxford University.

To show our appreciation of the various ways in which he helped us we invited him to supper in the cabin one night and with the aid of some excellent bottles of wine and a remarkable meal dished up by Henry — whose imagination and resource in the galley were a great asset whenever we entertained visitors — the evening developed uproariously and lasted well into the next morning. Coelho told us afterwards that he enjoyed the first half so much that he did not mind being unable to remember what happened in the second half. He came back the next day and asked for some of our songs to be written down for him so that he could sing them to his wife. Rather horrified, we made a discreet selection and hoped for the best. He assured us his wife could not speak a word of English.

After a visit to the Dezertas, a high, razor edged range of rocks just south of Madeira, with a local party in a doctor's motor boat, we put to sea again, this time our stores fortified by the gift of a case of delicious Madeira wine from Henry's University friend, who seemed to be Lord of the Island. For many weeks afterwards this wine was a great joy to us after munching our corned beef and biscuits.

We headed south for the desolate Salvages, intending to land there if the weather proved suitable.

It is much easier to get under way from an ocean island like Madeira than to get to sea out of an Essex creek. You just set your sails, drift out of the lee of the island into the wind track, and away you go. In fact, ocean cruising is a lot easier

Great Piton Island showing its highest point, the 177 foot Hart Hill.

than many people imagine, once you have got used to the long passages and mastered some primitive ideas on celestial navigation. Most of it is a matter of common sense, provided you are some sort of seaman to start with.

Our jolly old friend Coelho came off in a motor boat to wish us goodbye. He seemed to thoroughly enjoy himself puffing and blowing on sheets and halliards (''It's a long time since I've done any of this'') for he had served his younger years in schooners and square rigged ships. His final entreaty was that we should write to him from every port, first sending him a card from Great Salvage Island. This island is uninhabited but there is a letter box there which had been hewn out of the rock in ancient times. Anyone anchoring under the lee and able to effect a landing would collect letters and post them at the next port or else leave some to be picked up.

Gently and pleasantly we sailed to the southward, basking in the sun, a lazy swell pitching us on our way. Our bellies filled with luscious fruits and wines of Madeira, we gave ourselves up to the laziest passage I have ever made. We did nothing but cook, eat and steer; and in the cool of the evening sat round the quarter deck singing songs and playing tunes on an old melodeon. Henry, our star cook (we always looked forward to meals when it was his turn) devised seven different ways of dishing up corned beef without having it ''raw'' from the tin. His evening meals, accompanied by a glass of wine, were something which I can still remember with pleasure.

We left Funchal, with its cobbled streets, bullock-pulled skid carts, dull cafes and outlying ''goat and sheep'' villages on June 1st and on the morning of June 3rd saw the great gaunt rock which is called Great Salvage, principal of the little group of rocky islets — home of seabirds and whitened by their droppings. Miles away we could hear the breakers thundering on the cliff face and as we sailed round to the lee side it was obvious that there was no hope of anchoring and hazardous (to say the least of it) to make a landing in a small boat. And with the rollers breaking so high all round the island it would be doubtful, if we got ashore, whether we would be able to get off again.

So after jilling around for a while in the faint hope of spotting a quiet beach, we were forced to abandon the idea of posting our letters in this God forsaken dot on the chart. But just to the south lay Great Piton Island, with rocky Little Piton to the west of it; so we decided to run on and try our luck there. As far as we knew Great Piton was also uninhabited but on hauling round into the lee of the rocks we could see several open boats drawn up on the beach of a small sandy cove.

There was much better shelter under Piton than there had been at Great Salvage, and even though Sinclair confessed afterwards that the place scared him, we finally found a reasonable berth in eleven fathoms and let go the anchor with buoy and tripping line. We kept the mainsail set as it was obviously no place to lie very long. The small boat was launched and Henry and John rowed Sinclair ashore. I agreed to stay on board in case the anchorage proved untenable, probably because I was the only member of the crew with sufficient brute force to get the *Quartette* underway single handed if necessary. But the *Quartette* never seemed quite as big to me as she did to them because when I was young I had been to sea in a 350 ton barquentine with a total crew of four (skipper, cook, mate and myself) and later in 250 ton barges when the entire ship's company comprised just skipper and mate.

However, the anchorage proved better than we thought and during the late afternoon (it was three o'clock when we let go) the wind eased and the swell died down so they came back for me in the boat and Henry took over the anchor watch.

They had found on shore a colony of ten Spanish fishermen who had at first treated them with great hostility and suspicion because they thought we were Portuguese police come to turn them off the island. This desolate archipelago belongs to Portugal and these Spaniards were really trespassers. Apparently they came there every year from the Canary Islands to catch and salt seasonal fish. They and their boats were brought to Piton by a schooner and left there for about two months.

We landed at the tiny cove where the main colony was established. They lived in small huts with about four feet of headroom and built of stones, rocks and scrub. These were their only shelters. It was certainly a primitive settlement and as far as we could tell they lived as one might have expected Stone Age settlers to live. There were four women, one of them fairly old but the other

Fine weather watch in the Doldrums. John Bell becalmed at the *Quartette*'s tiller.

three young, bronzed and handsome. It was noticeable how the men kept at a distance from us.

The menfolk were typical Spaniards, lean and swarthy. Their leader, a stocky, bow-legged individual, explained by signs that they all came from the lesser known Canary Islands. He himself was from Lanzarote. He was greatly relieved to find that we were English and not Portuguese and did his best to explain how they caught, dried and salted the fish. We also saw limpets drying in the sun. All their fishing was done with two boats and a seine net and the salt was obtained from saltpans on the windward side of the island, salt left there by the breakers.

Although none of the others made any attempt to communicate with us and stood sullenly aside, the old man became quite voluble. We understood but little of his conversation, partly because his garlic flavoured breath was so vile that it was overwhelming even when standing to windward of him. John commented that to allow him to get to windward of us would have been certain death because the evil-smelling odour was supplemented by frequent, large and jelly-like expectoration which made a sinister pattern on the hot sand.

Escaping his attention, we made a tour of the island (about a mile right round) climbing to the top of Hart Hill, which is 177 feet at the highest point, the rest being nothing but low rock and scrub-covered sand. On the eastern side of the island we found another small camp of three men who regarded us with even more sullenness and suspicion than those we had first met. In fact, their demeanour was definitely ugly and had not the old ''chief'' come hurrying after us to explain to them who we were I am not quite sure what the outcome of our visit would have been. Even after being told who we were they followed us in a menacing manner until we were well clear of their camp, which we assumed to be the bachelor quarters.

I wondered afterwards that if these obviously primitive people had attacked and despatched us, robbed our ship and sunk her in deep water, it would have been a very long time, if ever, before the British Government ever came to hear of it. "Lost at sea" would probably be the verdict.

We spent about a couple of hours altogether, roaming and exploring the rocks and beaches, after which we agreed to allow the old "chief" and two other islanders to come aboard the *Quartette*, making sure that we were not outnumbered and politely discriminating against the gentlemen from the bachelor quarters.

We spent a distressing half hour with the old man's breath in our cabin, taking turns to go out on deck for a breather, and presented him with some fresh fruit, odd lengths of rope and a few bits of wood which they seemed to prize more than anything. We found several other items missing after they had gone — a frying pan, a pair of plimsols and one or two shackles. Apparently these had been slipped into their boat while the old man had kept us occupied in trying to understand him in the cabin. He shook hands heartily all round, releasing each of us before we became overpowered, but the other two were as sullen as ever and looked as though they would be glad to see the back of us. Which they did at six o'clock in the evening, when we set sail for the Canaries.

As we sailed away John advanced the far fetched, though not impossible theory, that the Piton islanders were all the old man's family and that he had been expelled from his native land because in so small a space the rest of the population could no longer suffer the smell of his breath. Being brought up with it, his own family could tolerate it but even three of them lived a little way apart. Well, perhaps John was right.

Shortly after leaving Piton we sighted the great peak of Tenerife, the 12,000 foot Pico Teyd, at a distance of 112 miles. This is a phenomenon which is not unusual in these latitudes and the pilot instructions for the Canary group mentions that the peak is frequently visible from 100 miles away. Even so, it gives you a peculiar sensation to see a snow capped mountain-top up in the sky ahead and nothing underneath it, not even a cloud. But at least it provided a good check on our compass and no-one could doubt that we had laid off the right course.

Because some of the crew had arranged for mail to be sent to Las Palmas, we made straight for there, anchoring in the beautiful harbour of La Luz and making excuses for frequent trips ashore to gaze upon the amazingly handsome senoritas who, on Sunday afternoons, promenade in the main thoroughfare with a grace, dignity and composure which earned the admiration of we barbarous northerners. Their chaperons were never far away.

The *Discovery* in East India Dock, birthplace of the *Quartette*'s ocean-going cat, Disco.

Even Disco, the cat, who had so far survived the voyage pretty well apart from a couple of fits in Madeira, tried to get ashore by leaping over the side. Sinclair and I rescued her by torchlight as she clawed desperately at the ship's side. When picked out of the water she continued her stroke strongly in mid-air and was still swimming hard until placed in safety on deck.

One evening, a little German boat named the *Zugvogel*, from the Hamburg Sailing Club, came into the harbour and we signalled them to tie up alongside us. This they did, and her crew proved to be a young couple named Mr and Mrs Furster, who were on their way to South America but were prepared to settle down anywhere if they found a country to their liking.

Of course, we had them aboard to supper in our cabin and we talked long into the night of ocean breezes, cruising boats, ports to make and ports to avoid, and all the day to day (perhaps I should say month to month) problems of the deep sea wanderer.

Their boat looked very small compared with the *Quartette*, being only 28 feet long, with a very small cabin. Her limited accommodation was divided into two — a comfortable double bed on one side and cooking facilities on the other. She was double ended and rigged in simple sloop fashion.

After a few days at La Luz we sailed across to Tenerife, averaging about seven knots all the way. We got under way at 6 am and let go under Tenerife, in the harbour of Santa Cruz, at four in the afternoon. The place looked very familiar to me and it did not seem almost two years since I had been there in the little cutter *Thelma* en route for the West Indies.

There is a brief entry at Tenerife in my daily journal which says ''Met many old friends'' and in this way several days passed very pleasantly. Sinclair, John and I also indulged in long day rambles out over the hilly countryside, sometimes in company with our friend Francisco Talavera, one of the port pilots. He took us up Pico Ingles one afternoon and stood us a wonderful supper in a little white, stone built country inn — the cost of a magnificent meal for four hungry men being five pesetas (about three shillings). And the wine — we don't know what wine is in England! Henry never accompanied us on these long tramps because he hated walking and said he always looked upon it as an obsolete form of progress. So it gave him a peaceful day aboard to do his letter writing.

Talavera had been a pilot in the Canary Islands for many, many years and told us that he spoke eight languages. "But not in full", he added. "Only port, starboard, ahead, astern and stop. Other words I do not know."

The little German *Zugvogel* from Hamburg, in La Luz harbour, Las Palmas.

CHAPTER EIGHT

White Man's Grave

IT WAS June and a bad month for the North East Trades. Also it was the hurricane season in the West Indies and by all accounts the islands were getting more than their usual share of cyclonic storms. So Sinclair and I agreed that our best course was to sail south to Cape Verde islands, thence to the West African coast and use the monsoon winds to get across the Equator to the South East Trades. We could then cross the Atlantic south of the line, calling at some little known islands which lie close off the African mainland as a jumping off point. Possibly we might break the passage to America by stepping ashore at Ascension Island or possibly Trinidada, the crab-ridden island explored by Frank Knight and his venturesome crew in the *Falcon* — one of the pioneer ocean cruises.

It was very grand and pleasant to sit in the old *Quartette*'s cabin, with a chart of the whole Atlantic held down by milk tins on the table, and dismiss a thousand miles or so of salt water with a mere sweep of the forefinger and read out in a detached manner the odd names of un-heard of places which appeared to be in our wind track. Time didn't matter much. A month here or a month there was only by the way. This is one of the joys that the poor old week-end and holiday yachtsman can never indulge in.

So we sailed away from sunny Tenerife on an 830 miles passage to St Vincent and a good start we had, too! The trades blew really hard and the old trawler averaged nine knots for a couple of hours as we cleared the land. The seas were high but regular and the *Quartette*, proving her beautiful underwater lines, pitched easily on her way.

Without incident, we made the Cape Verde Islands, where the last British square-rigger, the *Garthpool*, was wrecked, and we had to jill about off St Vincent in paltry airs before sailing gently to the anchorage, bringing up near some lighter roads where a stock of coal was kept by Cory Limited. It was charted as a "regular coaling station".

I had read and heard of the terrific squalls which periodically sweep down from the cliffs, so before allowing the crew to sample the delights of the hot and barren shore, I had them lay off a heavy kedge anchor on our best bass warp and chain. Feeling safe, we all turned in that night without setting an anchor watch. About 3 a.m. we were awakened by a sudden roar of wind accompanied by a terrific downpour of tropical rain, hammering the decks like pebbles. Then

The author acted as crew's barber, the agreed rate being one pint of beer per haircut.

there was a loud, sharp bang like a gun going off. I rushed up on deck in my underpants. Over the bow our main anchor chain hung straight up and down. A quick turn on the windlass and it came up without effort. The chain was broken. The kedge warp was now taking all the strain and I gingerly eased away on it so that the *Quartette* rode to the full scope. By this time Henry was with me and took careful bearings of objects on shore to enable us to check our position in case of dragging. While he was doing this, John and I got the mainsail gaskets off ready for an emergency getaway should the kedge fail us. By this time the rain suddenly ceased and we lay in a deathly calm. Sinclair put his head out of the scuttle hatch and asked "Is anything wrong?" Henry, being nearest, explained to him, rather tersely, I thought: "We parted the bower chain but the mate is holding her on the kedge warp."

Soon after daylight a lot of small negro boys came swimming round to dive for pennies in the clear still water. They were jolly little chaps in spite of looking half-starved and I asked them if they could dive to the bottom of the harbour and make a stout rope fast to our main anchor so that I could recover it. The news went round like wildfire and in a matter of moments the *Quartette* was surrounded by a swarm of expert divers of all ages ranging between eight and fourteen years. They were not without intelligence! They said they could not see copper pennies deep down, but if we threw silver coins overboard they could follow them down to the depth at which our anchor lay. It took a lot of sixpences to locate the anchor (I think they knew where it was all the time), but one of the bigger boys said he would take the rope down to make it fast. This he did and we soon had the anchor up on the windlass. As he seemed to be the sort of boss-boy, I gave him half-a-crown extra. Of course, they all wanted half-crowns then but I hardened my heart and told them to clear off in seaman's language, which they did quite happily, laughing and shouting with their mouths full of sixpences. They all looked very skinny and in need of good nourishment.

Sinclair was ashore so the three of us set about heaving all the bower chain up on deck, turning it end for end, and shackling it on afresh. The broken part had several worn links about three fathoms up from the anchor but the rest, which had been the inboard end, was as good as new. I had burned all the rust off at Whitstable and dipped it in hot tar.

Imagine my dismay, therefore, when Sinclair came back from the shore in Cory's launch with sixty fathoms of new chain which he had purchased from the company at a price which would have kept me in beer for the rest of my life. What a waste of money; what a waste of time and labour! Wearily, Henry and I shackled on the new chain. Then we went ashore and took part in a beer-drinking competition with some lads of Cory's coal staff. I think we won.

Glad to see the back of St Vincent after three days of its benighted harbour, we set sail for Sierre Leone, caring little about its reputation as ''the white man's grave'' after our experience in the Cape Verdes, although perhaps I give scant credit to the group if I do not mention that one of the islands has some green vegetation on it and there is an extinct volcano — the one that Drake's men saw when they sailed round the world. They thought at the time that the Earth might be flat, in spite of what the gallant Francis told them, and that they were in danger of sailing off the edge into hell, the glow and sparks of which (coming from Fogo Isle) could plainly be seen at night. Theirs was no mean courage to sail on and chance it!

Freetown was to be our port, and it seemed a handy place for our purpose. But no-one realised that at the time that we were innocently sailing towards the place, it was just commencing its rainy season. But we learned all about rainy seasons when we got there.

The distance is only 810 miles but we lost the trades on the eighth day out and drifted into the Doldrums. We wallowed in the heat for a couple of days and the only diversion apart from the everlasting job of renewing chafing gear aloft, was when the German steamer *Ubena* came close and dipped her flag to us. We replied and all her crew lined the rail to give us a cheer.

Then the rain came.

I learned in Madeira that in England we do not know what good wine is like. I learned in West Africa that we do not know in England what real rain is. It's no matter of a shower or steady drizzle. It's a continuous drenching downpour. All seafarers on the British coast are familiar with the torrential, blotting-out rain squalls we get with thunder storms. Well, in a West African rainy season it goes on like that all day!

At first we revelled in it, having had a surfeit of hot sunshine. All hands turned out with bars of soap and had a beautiful shower bath. I had not seen the *Quartette's* crew look so clean and hygienic before. Clothes were brought out and we all had a regular old English washing day.

Only Disco the cat showed a true appreciation of the rainy season. After a wet five minutes in the sand box he retired to my bunk and slept steadily for a couple of days. (By now it was obvious that we must give up calling Disco ''she.'')

On the twelfth day at sea we sighted land, but having had no sights for over 48 hours owing to the rain we did not identify it until the following morning during a lull in the downpourings, having been becalmed nearly all night. It proved to be the jungle covered Isles de Los, which boast a lighthouse, and proved to be a sure check on our position.

Next day we were off Freetown, becalmed again, and the following morning entered the River Rokel and anchored in Susan's Bay. Here we unbent the mainsail, which had flogged a cloth out of the leach in the rolling calms of the doldrums, and I took it ashore to a native boat-house to put in a new cloth and leech rope. Because of the enervating effect of the heat and damp the job took me longer than expected but my close contact with negro riggers, who used the shed, was amusing, informative and at times (when their lady friends visited them in the afternoons) quite shocking.

We could not have picked a more interesting anchorage because it was here that the native canoes, with their crude triangular sails, used only for fair winds, came to land their strange cargoes from Bullom Shore and the up-river regions. Strange people, they seemed, beating their tom-toms, dancing on a midship ''platform'' and keeping the Headman cool with great sunshades and fans as he sat aft in all his majesty. One canoe came alongside one evening when I was alone on deck and I was offered a wife in exchange for a case of corned beef: but after one look at the proferred wife, who had no say in the matter, I could not bring myself to part with the corned beef, of which I had always been very fond. Had she been one of the beauties of Las Palmas it might have been a different matter.

Freetown is full of interesting people, both black and white. Among the negroes it was soon easy to distinguish between the coastal tribes and the traders from up-country. I was greatly impressed by the tall, intelligent, distinguished-looking Hausa men who strode through the streets in their flowing Mohammedan robes, obviously regarding the local inhabitants with a haughty disdain.

Although Freetown appears to be a reasonably civilised and organised community, I was told that it happened to be situated on the borders of the old

Temne and Menzie tribal territories. For centuries these two tribes had fought bitter wars and even in these days still keep to their own part of the town. I asked one or two black men from other tribes if there was any real enmity between the Temnes and the Menzies nowadays and their answer was the same — that they would be at each other's throats within a fortnight if ever the white man left Sierre Leone. The older white settlers said the same.

Every white settler has a native watchman to guard his house against thieves. Tom Maloney, the genial easy going Irishman in charge of the local power house, explained that if you live in a Temne district you have a Menzie watchman and vice versa. It would be useless to have a Temne watchman in a Temne district. "You might as well not have a watchman" he said. So the tribal rivalry is at least some use to the white boss.

One very interesting chap who came aboard to tea one day was an English Channel-islander, named Molyneux, agent for a big firm who bought palm kernels from the natives. Sometimes he went 200 miles inland to purchase his palm kernels and arrange for their transportation to the coast. He told us that once while staying at a lonely bungalow up in the bush he was trapped in the

Sierre Leone. Native canoes setting sail in Rokel River. The "mast" is the small bent spar amidships and the triangular sail is thrust up on long bamboo poles by brute force. The sail is only for running before the wind. If there is a head wind the canoe is propelled by six young boys on each side at the fore end.

Quartette with a light wind from astern.

lavatory by a Mamba snake, the deadliest of all the local species. The lavatory was a little way away from the house and the snake got between him and the door. For a time he sat perfectly still and silent until the snake settled down again. Then Molyneux gave a shout which fortunately attracted the attention of some of his native ''boys'', who guessed immediately what was wrong and came running to the rescue. Alarmed, the snake rose up again to strike but before it could do so the negroes had ripped off the roof and hauled the white man up to safety, much relieved but looking somewhat undignified so far as his attire was concerned.

Molyneux had considerable admiration for the up-country native. ''He's a stout fellow; honest and faithful. But you must learn to know him.''

Another character we met was a rumbustrous old sea-dog from Hartlepool named Capt. Bowles. He piloted ships from Freetown up the dangerous Sherboro River and Lord help anyone, black or white, official or unofficial, who got in his way. He despised all the terrors of the climate — malaria, cholera, blackwater fever and such like — as things people catch if they're afraid of them. He had been pilot there for seven years, ignored all the customary precautions such as injections and quinine, and claimed that he was as fit in Sierre Leone as he had been back home in Hartlepool.

One interesting thing I learned from the Englishmen there was that the natives sucumbed to the climate much quicker than the white people, showing no resistance once they were taken ill with the prevalent fever. There was one white man we met who had lived in the ''white man's grave'' for seventeen years and looked a picture of hardihood and health. He was a Frenchman named Martroi who had lost all his known relations in the 1914-1918 war and in his grief had sought solace in the adventures of the African bush. He had never taken a holiday out of the climate, as most Europeans do. The usual procedure is to go home for three to six months every two years, but Martroi thought this did more harm than good and that it was best to keep in the same climate and thus become hardened to it.

We were a fortnight off Freetown, by which time I had finished the mainsail and patched up a big, light weather jib which had seen its best days. Henry used to call it the "gruyere" jib because it had so many holes in it. But it served us well on occasions. It was with this remarkable triangle of patches set on the bowsprit end that we sailed gently out of the Rokel River one morning and set off on a long distance coasting passage to the island of Fernando Po, 1365 miles away, and situated in the Bight of Benin.

No-one aboard the *Quartette* knew anything about Fernando Po. No-one had ever been near the place. But everyone voted to go there. The southwest monsoon blew that way, and the Guinea Current flowed that way, so it would be an unusual cruise (in contrast to the West Indies and Pacific jaunts undertaken by so many ocean yachts). As we had plenty of time there could be no argument against making a passage there.

We were glad to get to sea again and fill our lungs with good salt air after the humid heat of Sierre Leone. It was windward work to start with but the old *Quartette* plugged away comfortably and steadily just as though she was on her old trip out to the Dogger Bank. We got a good offing because we could then settle down to deep-sea watches and routine without having people's sleep disturbed with coastal pilotage, soundings, extra chart work and so on. But on the third day out, we ran into a real snorter and as dusk came, had to haul down a reef in the mainsail — the first time we had had to reef since leaving England.

These hard blows are short lived in this part of the world and so we saw no object in hammering away, although she would have kept pegging to windward had we chosen to force her. But instead we set a small jib and hove her to for the night. With the jib in the middle (both sheets tight) and the foresail to the mast, there was no need for a helmsman and she looked after herself for the first two watches, the would-be helmsman making himself comfortable in the shelter of the companion hatch and having a brew-up of tea or cocoa when he felt time hanging on his hands. We let the foresail draw at the end of the "graveyard watch" so that she began to jog ahead again, and before dawn we let go the weather sheet of the jib. When I came on deck again in the forenoon Henry was at the tiller easing her over the worst ones and making good about seven knots. He was a good steersman and could be left alone on deck in any weather. He was also my principal helpmate in the numerous "bosun" jobs to be done, both alow and aloft.

By the next day the latitude sights showed that we were well below Africa's western bulge and so with some relief we turned left and squared her away. Once her sheets were off she covered 410 miles in three days, our best noon to noon run being 181, with the aid of the Guinea current. "Worth a guinea a mile", John said. Sailing was easy then, and everyone was happy and cheerful. The only rotten job I had was to go out on the gaff end when we wanted to re-set the topsail because the sheet had chucked a slack bight over the end of the spar. But I was quite pleased to find that I could still do these monkey tricks.

I feel sure that the ability to clamber about in a ship's rigging (apart from any natural agility) is a matter of early training. Lads in sail who used to show any reluctance about going aloft used to be forced to go up and even compelled to stay up there longer than the others, masthead work being found for them sufficient to last all day. Before long they were just as good as those who went up without any hesitation. Mates of sailing vessels didn't psycho-analyse youths who showed any sign of fear or trepidation.

In the home trade craft we used to be made to "go round the mainsail", starting at the mast, up to the throat, out to the gaff end, down the leech rope and finally along the boom. Once you had done this on a big schooner's mainsail there were not many places aloft you were unfamiliar with.

Later, when I became master, I used to make any new lads do the same, and I noticed that those who did it at the first time of asking invariably became good seamen. I made it a rule that they got no extra money until they could go round the mainsail, stow a topsail, steer to windward and by compass, tie a bowline and scull a boat (one oar, I mean). Up to the 1930's they were entitled to the princely sum of thirty shillings a week and their grub, plus five bob a cargo. But power ships have changed all that. Lads who can take hatches on and off and make a decent pot of tea will soon become "A.B.'s" earning big money.

In the *Quartette* I discovered that monsoon winds are very different from trade winds. They may blow pretty consistently as far as direction is concerned but they do not give the pleasant sailing conditions of the blue-water routes. There are squalls, calms, thunderstorms, rain and sometimes cold nights. There was no urge to close the land as whenever we got a glimpse of it in the distance it always seemed to be shrouded in rain; and we had seen enough rain in Sierre Leone to last us the rest of the cruise. We got a few heavy showers out at sea but nothing like what they seemed to be getting on shore.

There was no expert navigation required to find the island of Fernando Po. We were on its latitude for days and days before seeing it and, the weather falling light and fickle, there was no fear of rushing past it in the dark. On the morning of our sixteenth day out from Freetown we sailed slowly up to the anchorage off Santa Isabel, which is the town and capital of the island.

Santa Isabel with its imposing cathedral spires looks an important place from the seaward but when you get ashore you find that, apart from the cathedral, there is very little else. It reminded me of a tropical edition of Harwich, which looks quite a place from offshore but can be walked round in just over five minutes.

It was a pleasant spot and not greatly affected by the mainland rainy season. In the hills not far out of the town live giant baboons, antelopes, flying foxes (a sort of large bat) and to the south are some three thousand head of cattle tended by natives. Most of the workpeople come from Calabar but the land and property owners are the native tribe of Bubis, from whom the big English companies purchase cocoa. One day while walking on the outskirts of the town, John and I came across a hut camp on a grassy hill, inhabited by men who were heavily painted, scarred and tattooed. These were the Pamwais, a most primitive tribe from the Cameroons, who came over to the island each year to sell skins. Nearly all the local natives were afraid of them and did not go near them after dark. Some said the Pamwais still "chop man beef" and whether this was true or not the islanders were not taking any chances.

We stayed at Fernando Po for a fortnight. By this time our cruise had been going on for four months and the reader might well inquire if we suffered from any crew troubles so unfortunately frequent in many ocean voyages of this nature. I will not say we were free from them but such irritations as arose were always in port and never at sea. Considering we were an ill assorted four we endured each other's eccentricities pretty well: and in achieving this much credit is due to Long John's dry humour and easy going nature. John never professed to be a crack seaman but he was always willing and the easiest chap in the world to get on with. I have come to the conclusion that on a long cruise a man who is difficult to get on with must, to compensate, be a first class seaman and in this way hold the respect of the others. If he is no great shakes as a seaman then he needs must be a willing and likeable companion. But the man who is neither a good seaman nor a likeable companion had better either stay ashore or cruise single handed.

While at Fernando Po we had a request from a young English mission school teacher named Wilfred Markham, who wanted to join us for the trans-Atlantic

Santa Isabel, capital of the island of Fernando Po.

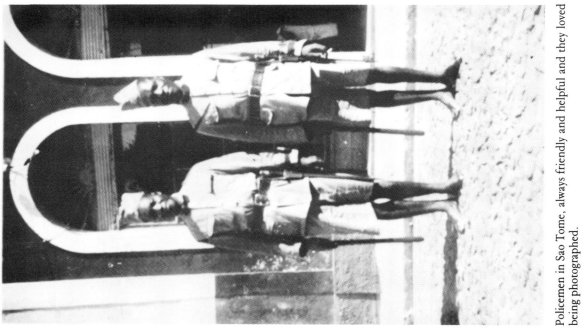

Policemen in Sao Tome, always friendly and helpful and they loved being photographed.

Miss Tome, Beauty Queen of the island.

run. He was an interesting visitor aboard and told us much about the island, and its natives, but financial difficulties prevented him from coming with us. Probably the native lads were very pleased that he did not come with us as they thought the world of him. He was one of the few white people there who could mix and play with them without ever losing their affection and respect.

Markham told us that at one period he was having a lot of fruit stolen from his garden so he went to see the local witch-doctor and asked his advice. The witch doctor agreed to put a ju-ju in Markham's garden, which consisted of a cocoa pod on a stick with three cock's feathers stuck in the top. Once this had been placed in the garden all stealing stopped. By way of experiment, Markham secretly replaced this with a ju-ju of his own making, a much grander and more prominent affair, but very soon the fruit stealing began again and Markham told the witch doctor what he had done. Immediately the witch doctor made a fresh ju-ju and put it in the garden and again all stealing stopped.

"I think they trust me more than any white man here" Markham said, "and they confide in me quite a bit; but I've never been able to get an explanation about that ju-ju."

There are three other islands south of Fernando Po, Spanish and Portuguese owned, named Principe, Sao Tome (St Thomas) and Annabon. We decided to sail to Sao Tome because there is a safe anchorage there and good water, we were told. From there we could set out across the South Atlantic.

Our passage from Fernando Po was a succession of calms and head winds which sometimes blew up into something more than a fresh breeze. While we were on this passage I think the crew began to show the effects of the West African climate. Sinclair, who was remarkably fit and tough for a man approaching sixty, looked pallid and ill. Henry caught a bad cold and Long John confessed to feeling out of sorts and off his food. I was fortunate enough to be exempt from these complaints.

With a fair slant we should have been at Sao Tome in three days but for the whole passage we were plagued with head winds and a foul current. After seven days beating slowly to windward we sighted the island of Principe in the early morning and by noon raised the Brothers, three desolate rocky islets to the south of Principe. We passed fairly close to the Brothers but could see nothing on them but birds and birdlime. That night I devised a hook and caught a fat bonito which we cut up into steaks for breakfast — a welcome change of diet except for Long John, who was violently ill if ever he tasted fish of any sort.

We were nine and a half days making Sao Tome and found it a splendid, smooth water anchorage. With the help of hired natives, we gave the ship a coat of paint, laid in a fresh stock of food and water, overhauled rigging and sails, and generally prepared for a voyage across to Rio de Janeiro, intending to call at Ascension if convenient (that is if we could find it and if the anchorage was tenable.)

In our spare time we sampled the joys of the shore, tasting some more exquisite Portuguese wine with our cheerful hosts at the Agua-Izo plantation — a very modern place with splendid accommodation and a fine hospital for the native workers. Our hosts could speak no English and we had no Portuguese so we spent the whole evening saying ''Viva Portugal'' and ''Viva Ingleterra''. We certainly cemented the ancient alliance between our two countries and parted very good friends.

At last we were ready to sail and just before we hove up our anchor a motor boat came off with a gift from the local bank manager — a salted pig, four live rabbits, sacks of coconuts and carrots and six large stalks of bananas. With our own stock, plus iron rations, there was little danger of starvation between Africa and America.

Sao Tome Island right on the equator. Modern buildings and hospital at the Portuguese plantation.

CHAPTER NINE

Ascension Island

IT WAS the middle of September when we set sail from Sao Tome and the monsoon rains and squalls were easing off. Friends we had made on the island came off in a launch to bid us farewell as we trimmed our sails to a pleasant southerly breeze which was just sufficient to fill our heavy North Sea canvas. By nightfall this fell to a calm, leaving us rolling gently in a smooth topped swell. Much of this and I knew that my unending labours aloft with the chafing gear would soon re-commence.

In the morning we were still well in sight of the bush covered shores of the island, though since leaving our anchorage we had not spotted a sign of life or habitation. It was rather fascinating to gaze at the green jungle, which came right down to the water's edge, and speculate on the wild and primitive life we knew existed in the dark interior. We all thought it would be worth while edging inshore to a reasonable anchorage and landing by small boat — perhaps to be greeted by a giant baboon, a python or even a real African lion. In fact, Sinclair would have been very pleased if we had for he had been teaching schoolchildren for years and years about the wild life in the African jungle and having at last come to the tropics in his later years had not seen anything more vicious than a few mosquitoes. He seemed a trifle disappointed in this respect. But a sudden diversion made us forget about landing as a great column of water suddenly shot up close on our port side. It was a huge whale, the biggest we had seen, and as he (or she) came to the surface we saw that its back was covered with barnacles and marine growth like a piling under a seaside pier. It was surrounded with a great school of porpoises, circling and snorting like a pack of hounds round a hunted animal. Whether this was the case or not I do not know but we saw no sign of the porpoises attacking the whale. Perhaps they were just having a game with the old fellow, for he must have been very old to have collected all those barnacles. Twice the great animal broke surface within some fifty yards of the *Quartette* and we became a bit apprehensive lest he use our keel as a means of scratching his back. I have no doubt that he was big enough and strong enough to have caused the mysterious loss of the *Quartette* and her crew. But gradually his blowings and splashings got further and further away as a little breeze came and we were able to lay away to the westward, towards America.

In the South-east Trades on course for Ascension Island.

For days and days we were on the port tack, plugging away against winds between south and south west which blew lightly during the day but tended to freshen at night. Our noon to noon runs were pitiful, often only fifteen or twenty miles a day, for we could not lay far enough to the southward to get clear of the adverse Guinea current. It was 1300 miles from Sao Tome to Ascension and I began to be thankful that we had such a good store of food and water. Even so, with over three thousand miles of ocean before us our Captain insisted on washing up in fresh water and might even have treated himself to a fresh water bath had not the rest of the crew made determined objections. This was the one occasion at sea when ''crew trouble'' showed itself aboard the *Quartette* while she was on passage. But with some measure of diplomacy this rough spot was smoothed over and the watches went on in regular and seamanlike manner to which we had all become accustomed.

We four, and Disco the cat, were not entirely without company on this Transatlantic attempt. A mulatto at Sao Tome had presented us with a tiny, month-old she-kitten to keep Disco company, it now being definitely established that Disco was a he. This new kitten ate voraciously and far from having fits as Disco used to do, she so distended her stomach with food that she had to lie on her back and wait for it to subside. The two cats soon made friends and together they used to hunt the four rabbits round the deck in the evenings until their antics began to show the killer touch. Then we had to keep the rabbits permanently in the small boat, which, fisherman style, was lashed on the starboard deck.

On the first Sunday at sea I executed two of the rabbits and they were the basis of an excellent stew. On the following Sunday, the other two followed suit. I suppose it would have been only logical to have celebrated the third Sunday with the cooking of the two cats but we had become rather fond of old Disco and it would have been too much like cannibalism. But I have eaten curried cat in a Chinese restaurant and found it excellent — quite as good as chicken. The West Africans, too, I noticed, were very partial to a bit of cat flesh and one bushboy who had come aboard at Sao Tome had wanted us to give him Disco as a reward for doing one of his native dances on our quarter deck. This young negro had "sung" for us too — a series of belly grunts, expertly syncopated, sounding very much like a modern dance orchestra without the saxophones. In fact, in its own class, the bush-negro was, I thought, more skilful than the London Tin Pan Alley imitators.

After five days we got clear of the Guinea current and, according to our navigational reckonings, began to get a little help from the Equatorial current which, according to that much valued book "Ocean Passages of the World", flowed gently in our favour. But the tracy winds plagued us day after day and we were forced to bout ship several times, slowly turning to windward along the line of the Equator. I don't suppose there are many vessels which have crossed and re-crossed the Equator in this manner and there was a distinct strangeness in the weather conditions while sailing along the Line. At night it was quite cold, and I remember how on one graveyard watch I was at the helm making a long board across the Earth's waistline and quite glad to have donned two jerseys, woollen hat and leather seaboots just as if I was back on the English coast in wintertime. In the daytime the wind tended to souther and grow squally.

Long John thought it was a pity not to have some memento of these Equatorial tacks and one noon appeared on deck with an old medicine bottle. This he tied on a piece of spunyarn and carefully lowered over the side when Sinclair and I had taken sights and announced that we were right on the line. Drawing up his bottle full of water, John carefully corked it and regarded it with obvious satisfaction.

"There you are" he said proudly. "There's a bit of the Equator and I'm going to take that home and stand it on the front room mantlepiece. And when I tell people in West Mersea that I have sailed to and fro across the Equator three times a week I can say 'and if you don't believe me, there's a bit of the Equator in that bottle.'"

So John packed away his bottle-full of Equator among his belongings and I presume that this now adorns the new home he has since set up for himself in Tasmania.

In the calms the ship's gear still suffered from chafe in spite of the lead blocks and chafing gear I had contrived aloft. There seemed to be no permanent cure for it. The only solution I could think of was wire halliards and that would have meant installing crab winches and also a risk of wringing the masthead. Alas, I am prejudiced against mechanical things aboard a sailing vessel on a long voyage. Anything that cannot be repaired with a marline-spike, mallet or maul should in my opinion be discarded. I am not an experienced yachtsman and am by nature and upbringing suspicious of the engineering fraternity. But I'm hanged if I'd be pestered in mid-ocean with some of the fiddling little contraptions I have seen which need to be sent back to a watchmaker if they go wrong.

After ten days, our total progress towards Ascension Island measured less than three hundred miles. Then we suddenly found ourselves in the South East Trades. It was like coming out of a stuffy house into the fresh air. In a matter of two hours the sea became a lovely deep blue and the waves white flecked with the best of all sailing breezes. Flying fish shot across our bows and the comic little Portuguese men of war bobbed drunkenly in the troughs. Porpoises and magic coloured coryphaena kept us company. The canvas bellied out to a steady strain on the spars and rigging. No more chafe and slatting. Hour after hour, day after day, the *Quartette* bounded along at a steady seven knots or so. When Sinclair our Captain, tasting his first trade wind run, commented that he thought it was a monotonous sort of sailing I felt that indeed he must be a hard man to please. But that is all a matter of comparison. If you have had to earn your living in deep laden cargo vessels in the gales and fogs of northern waters, where a tight sheet or a kick of the foresail means a long passage with little reward, this trade wind sailing is a sort of Seventh Heaven. You know it will not freshen to a gale, you know it will not fall to a calm, you know it will stay fair. And all this time it is sunny and warm and the very sea itself is beautiful. If there is such a thing as a sailor's Valhalla then it must be something like this.

Each noon the runs were measured off — 149, 143, 157, 147 — and thus we ran the last 1050 miles to Ascension in seven days. We got onto the latitude of the island some fifty miles to the east of it and spotted the mountain one forenoon without any difficulty. On the morning of our seventeenth day out from Sao Tome we hauled under the lee of the land and came to anchor with a scope of 40 fathoms of warp and chain, having read of the dangers of heavy rollers.

A Cable Company friend in Sao Tome had sent a message to Ascension telling them of our coming, so no sooner was our mainsail stowed than a launch came off with two Englishmen and a crew of St Helenians, who performed the unskilled and semi-skilled tasks for the Cable Company station. The men in the launch advised us that there were not likely to be any dangerous rollers and offered a large mooring buoy near some landing steps. We soon hove up our anchor and sailed across the bay to the mooring, on which we lay safely for the six days of our stay there.

Talking to the St Helenian boatmen, they told me of their own island 700 miles away (the nearest land to Ascension) and described how much better a place it was to visit. It was a good anchorage, they said, plenty of fruit and food, and only one man to every seven women. Sinclair, being much older than the rest of us, didn't think it worth while going there. The St Helena men spoke excellent English without the slightest trace of dialect or pidgin. In fact, their

English was much better than one hears in most parts of England. I judged that they were very proud of their British nationality. Their ancestry is interesting, being descended from a mixture of Negro, British, French (some of their forefathers having belonged to Napoleon's entourage when he was exiled) and Malay. The reason for the infusion of Malay blood is that many years ago a ship put into St Helena with her Malay crew all sick of some dread disease, possibly scurvy. All were put ashore, and some died, but many recovered and, the ship having gone away, they settled on the island and took wives. But the result of this rather strange mixing of their races is a population of brown skinned, active and intelligent people of whom the menfolk, as is natural among island folk everywhere, are excellent boatmen and seamen.

About 200 St Helenians worked on Ascension and those I met impressed me by their politeness, good nature and high standard of intelligence. We found thirty English folk living in very English looking little houses, all being employees of the Cable Company, some having their wives with them. They visited each other for tea, had dinner parties, dances and bathing outings. It was just like being in England, except for the beautiful oceanic climate.

We spent six days at the island and everyone was most kind and hospitable. We would have lunch with one couple, tea with another, and all assemble at someone else's house for the evening. Everyone seemed to be on the best of terms and I was told that their social life was so pleasantly organised that there was never a sign of any back-biting, bad feeling or malicious gossip. It was, in fact, a model colony of English folk making the best of things on a tiny island nearly four thousand miles from home. It was thought that lunch at the bachelor's mess had better be left until the day before our departure and by the time that particular lunch was over I could quite understand the wisdom of our hosts' decision.

One day we climbed the island's 2,800 foot mountain and found at the top that there was plenty of green vegetation, nurtured by cloud moisture, although the lower levels were of arid rock and volcanic dust. There was even a farm on the mountain top, being looked after by a man named Robson who had been a warrant officer in the Navy. At one time the British Navy had completely

Trade wind trees on Ascension Island.

71

"Two boats" (one rotted away). How the Royal Navy marked the road miles from the shore in the days when it was H.M.S. *Ascension.*

occupied the island and in those days it was called H.M.S. Ascension. Relics of their stay could be seen everywhere and distances on the road up from the shore were marked by old Navy whalers sawn in half and stood upright in the ground. Thus, the first mile was "one boat", the second mile "two boats" and so on. According to the number of boats standing by the roadside you knew how many miles you were from the landing place. The navy men had also built a little church out of oil cans, complete with spire, in which the "Governor", Mr L. F. Bartlett (who at the time of our visit was manager of the cable station) used to hold a service on Sunday mornings. Everyone went.

While at Ascension the *Quartette* gradually acquired a lovely clean bottom, losing every trace of weed and barnacle. This was due to the efforts of hundreds of little black fish who act as sea scavengers and eat everything off a ship's bottom. So I can advise any yachtsman who is fed up with the weary business of beaching, scrubbing and scraping his boat to sail away to Ascension Island and have it all done by nature; free, gratis and for nothing.

In spite of all the stories of fearsome rollers to be experienced at Ascension (there are some grim warnings in the pilot book) we laid in calm water for the whole of our stay there.

Our little Portuguese kitten had been very ill aboard so we took her ashore and established her in the home of one of the English couples there. This left Disco master of his own sand-box again and he seemed much happier. He had not liked sharing it with the little foreigner.

Of all the 6,000 odd miles our cruise had so far taken us, we all voted that the call at Ascension was the most pleasant. Perhaps we had grown a bit weary of the steamy landfalls of West Africa and of the constant struggling with foreign tongues and pidgin English. Anyway, it was very agreeable to be able to relax into English ways, English customs and the English language; to understand and be understood without having to make signs and draw pictures of what you meant to convey.

Thus refreshed, we sailed away, fearful that we might outstay our welcome, and all vowing that one day we would return. And so to sea again, with 2,000 miles of South Atlantic between us and Rio de Janeiro.

We were right in the middle of the trade wind belt at Ascension where even the trees and vegetation all grow slanting to leeward. Once the sails were well set we picked up a speed of about seven knots and in the first four days ran 530 miles. The wind was well on the port quarter and with everything drawing there was no danger of a gybe. My impression was that these south east trades blew much stronger than the north east trades and it was very rarely that our noon to noon runs fell below 120. The only discomfort was that as we edged south we occasionally got a southerly cross sea which broke the evenness of the trade swell and slopped across our low quarters.

We found that the tropical sun had opened our decks more than we expected and the only dry bunk in the ship was occupied by Sinclair. John, Henry and myself were all forced to shift our bedding to the hold, where we made ourselves comfortable on what had been intended for sail racks. The forecastle which had been built at great expense to house John and Henry became quite untenable. The midship decks remained tight and the hold was the driest place in the ship. It was also the airiest in the hot climates.

At the time when I abandoned my original bunk in the main cabin I had reached the stage when, after a half naked day-time existence, I had to don oilskins and sou'wester to turn in. I thought that then it was time to give it best. I beat a retreat to the sailracks.

As the pleasant days rolled by we took the opportunity to clean up the ship and got some painting done. Having ample food we fed like fighting cocks, taking it in turn to be cook for the day. Of course, Henry was always the author of the prime dishes and he took over Sinclair's share of the cooking. John had about two dishes which he worked alternately on his cook days so we always knew what we were going to get — something straight and simple. I had about four alternatives, including the traditional lobscouse, but Henry went in for elaborate affairs which took him nearly all day to prepare and would have been all the rage in a Soho restaurant.

As the trade wind held the gear steady I did not have to spend so much time aloft as on other passages and took the opportunity to set up the main rigging, renew servings, and take life more comfortably than heretofore. The only rotten job I had was when the upper cap of the topmast worked loose and I had to spend a wild half hour at the mainmast head manipulating a fourteen pound maul.

Quite a lot of flying fish landed on our deck and these were mostly handed over to Disco as they were too small to make much of a meal for us. In any case we thought fresh fish would improve his diet.

For seven days we bounded across the ocean, thinking we were going to make a really smart passage. We had read in "Ocean Passages" that where the south east trade peters out near the Brazilian coast we might expect a north east breeze, but during the first two days of our second week at sea the breeze shifted to the east and fell light, accompanied by an unholy southerly swell. One day was sheer agony, the gear crashing and slatting about for hour after hour. Twice the boom tackle broke but the peak vang held on and saved an enormous amount of chafe.

Henry and I hauled out the square foresail and boomed it out as a spinaker. While the wind was light it helped us to keep our daily runs over the hundred. But on the 10th day we were almost completely becalmed and the north east breeze we had hoped for did not materialise. All hopes of a quick passage faded away. We were still some 350 miles from the Brazilian coast. Rolling and slatting, the *Quartette* crept along her course, and on one day the noon to noon run by log was exactly seven miles. The distance covered was 21 miles, the current being in our favour.

It was while we were enduring this doldrum weather that Henry calculated it was our 100th day at sea (time in port not counted) so we celebrated as best we could with one of his special meals. On that day I harpooned a shark and when I cut off his tail, John had the brilliant idea that this should act as a very strong ju-ju. He had been very impressed with the witch doctor palaver while we were on the West African coast and on his instructions the bloodstained tail was hoisted to the topmast head, John mumbling incantations as it went aloft. For a few moments we all stood still, gazing over the oily swell to see what effect John's ju-ju would have.

And, lo and behold, over the water came a dark patch from the north east, spreading wider and wider as it neared our ship. It was a breeze; the first we had felt for 40 hours!

John wagged his head solemnly. "Very strong ju-ju", he said.

This "ju-ju" wind had not much weight in it but enough to push us along at 20-24 miles a watch as we neared the shoals of the South American coast. Once it blew up into a seven knot breeze and gave us quite a dirty night. But a dirty night in the *Quartette* only meant that the topsail had to come down, the little mizzen stowed and a medium jib set. This did not take very long and only very rarely did we have to reef the mainsail. When this breeze fell away we were almost becalmed and Sinclair, during his watch, sighted a steamship heading north. We reckoned that we were then only 210 miles from Rio and getting into the offshore shipping lanes. Running the deserted trade-wind routes, it is quite an event to see a steamship and we all turned out to see her lights.

It took us another two days to make that 210 miles, but the night before we arrived off the Sugar Loaf mountain which marks the entrance to Rio bay, we had a night of rain and squalls as though we were in the English Channel. It was cold, too. I had to abandon most of my watch below as Sinclair and Henry had tried to take the topsail in and there was a bit of a frap-up. Also I had to reef the mizzen. Sinclair never seemed to get the hang of handling a topsail, even after cruising all this way, and I suppose this is what comes of having a pole masted little boat when he was learning to sail.

On the morning of our 20th day out of Ascension we entered the harbour and were directed to a comfortable anchorage in Jurajuba Bay, off the Rio Sailing Club. This was an English club and its members were most hospitable. I think they were glad to have an English ocean cruiser visit them as they were rather overwhelmed by the much more numerous members of the German sailing club next door.

There were a vast number of Germans in Brazil at the time, many of them having emigrated there after their country's defeat in the First World War. We visited them one evening and found them a very cheerful, beer drinking crowd. One day we sailed up the 18 miles of harbour and visited the beautiful little island of Paqueta. This is one of those tropical spots which tempt you to give up striving and become a ''lotus-eater''.

Once we were invited to dinner at the English bachelor quarters, known as Chacara. It was a Saturday. Other members of the club said: ''If you get out of there by Tuesday, you'll be lucky.''

Sugar Loaf Hill, Rio de Janeiro.

Quartette in Rio harbour.

Well, when the bachelors of Chacara entertain, they go the whole hog. I got out of the front door on the Monday and had a walk round the house for a breath of fresh air but did not know my way back to the ship so went back in to inquire. So it *was* Tuesday, after all, when we finally got away.

Our days at Rio were happy ones indeed; but there was one sad thing about it all. John decided to go back to England. It is not my business to relate his reasons for leaving the ship but both Henry and I were very sorry to lose his company. Willing, cheerful and possessed of a deep sense of humour, he was a young man with whom you could live at close quarters without any danger of nervy ructions. Later he joined the Navy and served with distinction in sea engagements of the Second World War.

While at Rio we collected mail which had been accumulating there for five months so much of our spare time was spent answering letters. One member of the crew received a final demand for some Income Tax which was dated in England seven months previously. This he screwed up and threw down a Brazilian drain with a cynical laugh.

After John had sailed away in a big ship, we got ready for sea again. With only three of us we decided that the best watch keeping arrangement would be to do three hours each at the helm, the next man on watch being the one to be called out if help was required. This proved satisfactory and in moderate weather we all got a six hour stretch below.

We agreed to sail direct to the Demerara River, where Bully and I had made our landfall when we crossed the Atlantic in the 27 foot cutter *Thelma* some three years before. The distance from Rio is 2,875 miles and it is the longest coasting trip I have ever undertaken. We knew that for the first thousand miles we were likely to be faced with head winds but on an ocean cruise where time and distance matter so little a task such as this is taken on almost without a second thought.

After we left Rio, we heard no more of the little German boat *Zugvogel*, so her transatlantic voyage, made with a minimum of gear and comfort, sinks into the unwritten obscurity of many other of the early ocean voyages in open boats about which little is known. While most yachtsmen are familiar with the names of those who have written books about their exploits, few have ever heard of Captain Dow in the little 22 foot *Chance*, the two Polish lads in the obsolete racer *Zjawa*, and the young Dane who, coming south via Poole, Vigo, Rio and Buenos Aires, set off to round Cape Horn alone and was never heard of again. There are a number of others, too, who made excellent ocean voyages in tiny craft many years ago but who never received a line of publicity and are now practically unknown. Perhaps one day someone will collect information about these ocean cruising pioneers.

So it was goodbye to Rio de Janeiro — a good place for ocean cruisers and very different from the dreadful, fever-stricken dump it used to be in the heyday of the old square rigged ships. A very aged sea-faring friend of mine who finished his spare-rig sailing time as second mate of the old *Port Patrick*, told me once that he had seen as many as twenty two sailing ships lying to their anchors in Rio without a single man aboard any one of them. All the crews were down with yellow fever (for which the port had a very bad reputation), malaria or blackwater fever. Volunteers were called for from visiting ships and offered large bonuses to help form skeleton crews to sail the vessels away to healthier waters. In this manner, assisted by natives raked up by local crimps, the stricken ships were gradually got to sea — some in charge of men who had never before ranked higher than second mate.

Things are very different now in Rio, largely due to British and American influence. A modern city has risen up among the hovels (though many still cluster in the musty side streets) and if anyone so much as reports a single mosquito in the house a flying squad is rushed to the spot to dispose of it and any eggs it may have laid. Modern science and hygiene have completely erased the curse of one of the world's most dreaded fever ports.

Two days out from Rio, off Cape Fria, we ran slap into a whistling north easter. Being well offshore, and finding we could make no progress against it, we hauled down a single reef in the mainsail and hove-to on the port tack, slowly fore-reaching away from the land. The Portuguese named this Cape aptly enough for it was cold all right, although I don't know why it should be in these latitudes.

Sinclair got a lash in the eye from a halliard during the reefing operations and this incident, in addition to his feeling generally unwell at the time, put him out of action. Henry and I split up watches into the old four on and four off until the Captain was better. This was no hardship as most of the time while Sinclair was recovering we were hove-to with little to do but poke a head out of the scuttle hatch now and then to see if everything was all right.

After the first eight hours hove-to the wind increased to a real gale with heavy breaking seas such as one gets off the Longships back home. Henry and I reefed the mizzen and foresail and lashed the tiller very slightly a-lee and in this way the old boat rode as comfortably as any boat could be expected to do in such weather. We could still have our meals off the cabin table in a reasonably civilised manner, although Henry remarked that he could now see what was meant in the missionary calendar by a "moveable feast." We were still hove-to at breakfast time the next day but the squalls were less frequent and the seas less white on the crests. In the forenoon we let draw and started to edge to eastward. By the late afternoon we were able to shake the reefs out of the mainsail and foresail and get her round on to the other tack. On this tack the seas were more abeam and the *Quartette*, still riding like a duck, made some four knots to windward.

By the time we had picked up the land and put about once more the wind again increased to gale force. Down came the reefs again and for another twenty four hours we lay to a howling north-easter. But when this blow eased away the weather broke fine and it was not long before the topsail went up and we went ramping along, close hauled to a nice sailing breeze from about the north north west.

We kept on this tack for nearly a fortnight. It seems strange, compared with coasting in home waters, to spend a couple of weeks on one board and think to yourself "If there's no change in the wind during the next couple of days we'll chuck her round and pick up the land again." But progress was not easy and we had a lot of uncomfortable days. There was always a head sea.

I find that one of the entries in my private journal gives a fair description of this part of our voyage. It reads:

"Dec. 1st. At noon reached 15 deg 40. Now 13 days out of Rio and getting northwards better than expected. Otherwise we have had a lousy time. Gear given a lot of trouble. Main peak vang parted; boom guy parted; main peak cringle chafed through; mizzen sheet cleat broke; forward pin rail carried away; mizzen peak halliard chafed through; topsail tack downhaul parted aloft. All these things I have had to patch up and repair myself. Henry helps me all he can . . ."

The worst job was the mizzen peak halliard. A strand had chafed through on the gaff and it was no use trying to lower the sail down as the loose strand would have jammed in the block. So I had to spend an uncomfortably long time clinging to the gaff while I rigged up a temporary halliard and then turned the old one end for end and re-rove it with the sail still set.

There is another entry made that day, later in the evening.

"We are now on the edge of the south-east trades. Hoping to make Georgetown by Christmas." But the trades were spent and fitful.

One day we thought all our troubles were at an end and bowled along in fine style for several hours, only to find ourselves in a hazy calm. It was December 13th, our 25th day at sea, that we started to make real mileage and could, for the first time, slack off the sheets. The trade wind was south-east to east and only moderate but on a course north-north-west we had a favourable current on our quarter which pushed us an extra 18 to 20 miles a day. This brought our noon to noon runs up to near the hundred mark.

Alas; there was little joy to be found in this trip. Even when the wind favoured us our little cat Disco fell seriously ill. He had a fit and later patches of fur came off him. He ate little and even a tasty flying fish was left unfinished. We dosed him with vitamins A and D out of a bottle given to us by our Doctor friend of the Narrow Seas Club. Later Disco seemed a bit better but a couple of days later he had another fit and we found that he gone blind. He staggered around the cabin making pitiful noises, sometimes collapsing in an awkward heap.

We all agreed that the time had come to put him out of his misery. I tied his limp body to a couple of heavy iron bolts and pitched him over the side.

The Isle of Paqueta, a beauty spot 18 miles from the entrance to Rio harbour, where *Quartette* anchored for the night.

79

I was fond of old Disco. Ship-born, he was a true ship's cat if ever there was one, never having tasted life ashore. He lies buried in a sailor's grave in latitude 2 degrees north, lontitude 44 degrees 50 west, off the mouth of the Amazon.

With the death of this little black cat, luck left the *Quartette*. Nothing went right; the crew could not agree; the cruise was brought to an early close and the ship was sold.

I know it is foolish to be superstitious but at sea you tend to grow that way. When my old boat the *Thelma* was wrecked on Cocos Island we had sailed on a Friday. Another time when I sailed on a Friday the ship caught fire and sank and we had to jump into the North Sea on a dark and stormy night, of which I shall tell in a later chapter. A ship which killed a shipwright when she was launched killed two men afterwards and nearly had me. Hatches left upside down always worry me too and I always turn them the proper way up (just in case). I knew a barge skipper who did something he ought not to have done on the 13th day of the month and was blown to smithereens by a mine as soon as he put to sea. I think that perhaps the wind and the sea and the loneliness all tend to make you believe in illogical things. But after all, you can't prove everything by figures and science. As a little girl once said to me in a Suffolk lane, ''Grown-ups who don't believe in fairies only say so because they haven't seen one.'' And that's a good sound piece of Suffolk logic!

Even after we found our fair wind the weather was squally and unreliable. Sometimes there were several hours of calm. We had a glimpse of Pernambuco but after that the land was only a line of haze in the distance.

According to my journal, December 16th (our 28th day out of Rio) was another busy day.

''Stuck two new cringles in topsail without lowering it. Stretched and rove new jack stay. Re-stitched foresail bolt rope near sheet. Repaired and adjusted chafing gear. Cooked evening meal and washed up.''

The next day it rained hard with heavy squalls from right astern. The day's run reckoned up to 172 miles and there was another 570 to cover to reach the Demerara River. With a little good fortune now we felt fairly confident of reaching there by Christmas although after the death of Disco I was quite prepared to have a sprig of imitation holly stuck in a bit of corned beef, becalmed somewhere off the Guiana coast on the festive day.

The Guiana current was a great help, running at some two and a half knots in our favour, so that one day our noon to noon distance measured 212 miles. Soon the discoloured, brownish water from the Guiana rivers became visible and at last, on the 35th day out of Rio, we sighted what was, to me, the familiar sight of the Demerara Beacon, the lonely sentinel of the offshore flats where in the *Thelma* Bully and I had first tied up after 50 days crossing the Atlantic.

Christmas in Georgetown; with all the many friends who had welcomed me there before, both black and white. I dined once more with Georgetown's only yachtsman, the port doctor, Dr. Cochran, who had a remarkable "hubble-bubble" pipe — a sort of Heath Robinson affair which he set up on a stand and smoked after meals. There were several fathoms of it. Both the yacht and the pipe were a source of wonderment to the natives.

We decided to sail from Georgetown to Port of Spain, Trinidad.

Henry went home from Port of Spain, back to his native Cornwall. Our shipboard friendship grew, in years to come, into a permanent respect for each other. True to the ancient tradition of the Trefusis family, he was a gentleman and a seaman.

The *Quartette* was sold to a West Indian skipper to be converted for red snapper fishing. I never heard of her again. Sinclair took off to Canada to stay with his sister, leaving me with £55 to find my way home. I learned later he had sold the *Quartette* for £300.

I joined a local schooner as temporary mate, trading between Sinnimara and Demerara Rivers and up to Port of Spain, Barbados and Martinique. She only carried 170 tons and there were nine negroes in the forecastle. For me it was a do-nothing life of false dignity and rum. As soon as I had saved enough for the fare to England I booked a passage in the 30 year old Dutch ship *Crijnssen*.

It was back to the barges again, my ocean wanderings at an end — cattle cake for Yarmouth, coal for Margate, linseed for Southampton — it seemed as if I had never been away.

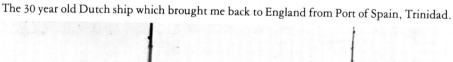

The 30 year old Dutch ship which brought me back to England from Port of Spain, Trinidad.

CHAPTER TEN

The Great Keadby Pig Census

L OADING coal at Keadby in the barge *Cambria* was never a dull affair. It is a remote village, about five miles from the steel town of Scunthorpe, and sits at the junction of the fast flowing River Trent and the Sheffield Canal.

The coal comes in ten-ton trucks. We generally took in what was called "Derby Washed Nuts", which meant that there was little or no dust. The trucks were shunted to an angled tip and the "washed nuts" cascaded into our hold like a black avalanche. Three local men did the trimming with heavy shovels and it would have done London dockers good to see those Lincolnshire men work. They would get under the side decks and allow themselves to be almost buried by the avalanche. Then we would see a flailing shovel appear, followed by a blackened face, all smiles — and not a cubic foot of stowage space was wasted. Skippers and mates might be justified in their bitter complaints of the way dockers worked (or failed to work) in the big ports, but no-one could ever complain about the way Keadby men loaded a ship. They asked for nothing other than their wages, but the "beer-money" we gave them was well deserved and willingly given. And they would help us to shift the barge in the roaring Trent tide to let the next ship take the berth.

Trent tides are not just an average ebb and flow. There is a bore about a foot high which comes rushing up in a white line over the fast out-going current. From away down the river one can hear the keelmen crying "Aegir — aegir", warning each other that the bore was coming and that they must stand by their moorings. Aegir is the old Norse word for a river bore, and no doubt that cry was heard along the Trent a thousand years ago. It is also spelt "eagre" or "eager", which is rather more Anglo-Saxon. Norman-French never intruded into the northern dialects.

One day the aegir nearly caused us a major disaster. The *Cambria* was safely moored at Keadby quay waiting to load and the main anchor was slacked down "stock awash", as was the custom when coming alongside to avoid any danger of it rupturing the barge. It would just swing underneath the fore-foot. But on this occasion the mate Nobby Lambkin had decided to clean and oil the windlass. To do this he had to put the "dogs" on the chain (a heavy iron claw) so that he could slack up the turns of chain on the barrel and spin the cog-wheels round. Before he had finished this task the aegir came rushing up the river and

Friends to sailormen. Albert and Lila Spriggs and ''Ikky'', the barman, at the *Friendship Inn*, Keadby.

we had to stand by our mooring ropes. The water rose with amazing rapidity and suddenly we realised that a fluke of the anchor had fouled the old wooden beams of the jetty below the surface. Within a few minutes the *Cambria* was pinned down by the head with her stern in the air. We ran to slack the anchor chain but could not as the dogs were still on and held bar taut by a strong dog-chain and shackle. We belted the dogs with a 14 pound hammer but to no avail. Down — down went the barge's head until the water was only a foot from the deck level. In desperation I rushed aft and got a can of lubricating oil, throwing the lot over the links where the claw was. The mate, a hefty Kentish lad, gave the taut anchor chain a mighty hammer blow. The dogs flew off, the anchor chain rattled out and, to our immense relief, the head of the barge reared up to its proper trim. It was a nasty moment and we might easily have lost the barge in that short time.

It was low water about mid-afternoon and I was still worried by the thought that our anchor was probably still embedded in a wooden pile near the bottom of the river. We slacked the mooring ropes and let the barge sheer a few feet off the quay. Gently we hove on the windlass, expecting to be brought up short when all the slack chain was in. But, lo and behold, without any hard heaving, the anchor came up clear. A sliver of rotten timber floated away downstream and we repaired to the *Friendship Inn* to rehabilitate ourselves. We needed a pint of good Lincolnshire ale and the landlady drew them up as she saw us enter the doorway. Her name was Lila Spriggs and to us seafarers she was the queen of all landladies. In her pub a sailorman short of money was never short of a pint. Nor was he ever short of a good meal.

Lila always "looked after my sailorboys." She had seen men off the ships and barges arrive red-eyed and weary after sleepless nights and heavy weather at sea. "Ikky" the barman would be sent aboard with a tray of pints and an invitation to "come up for breakfast." And if anyone had a bad word to say about sailors she would slap them down in our defence. Once someone saw a seaman walking along the towpath with a local girl and remarked "That chap has got a girl in London": to which Lila quickly retorted: "When you're a long way from home you've got to take what's handy."

Keadby was once described as a "row of cottages, three pubs and a coal shute." The folk there were close-knit, friendly and generous. Coasting seamen found the place a pleasant change from the evil docklands of the big ports. Social life concentrated on the three pubs, *The Friendship*, *The South Yorks* and *The Mariners* (which was a beer house only). At one time the landlord of the *South Yorks* was the foreman coal-trimmer as well.

In the days of rationing after World War II a householder was allowed to keep a pig and buy fodder for it provided he surrendered his bacon ration. But he had to be a registered pig-keeper. Everyone in Keadby kept a pig, sometimes two or three, but filling up forms on the matter did not seem to merit their attention. There was some alarm in the village therefore when news filtered through from the surrounding countryside that a Ministry of Food official was on his way to check up on the pig-keepers. There were quiet, low-toned conferences in the pubs and among knots of men leaning on the lock gates. It was evident that some plan was being hatched to disrupt officialdom.

"Ikky", the *Friendship* barman, also worked as the railway bridgeman at Keadby Halt, and he was deputed as lookout for the unwanted man from the Ministry. On the appointed morning, he phoned through to Lila "he's now getting off the train". Everyone let their pigs out and soon they were all snorting around the village, cropping greenery off the verges and enjoying their new-found freedom. Keadby seemed to be populated by pigs and only occasionally could a human being be seen leaning on a gate or sitting nonchalantly at a pub door. The Ministry official asked anyone he met "who do these pigs belong to?" All he got was a blank look, a shrug of the shoulders and a shake of the head. No-one knew who they belonged to. There were about fifty of them roaming about and wandering in and out of peoples gardens. They were "shooed" out with a show of annoyance and indignation. "I don't know where they come from or who they belong to," was the usual answer the official was given.

Tired and perspiring, the Ministry man retired to the *Friendship* for a sandwich and a beer. Lila looked sympathetic. Her London customer was irritable and despondent. It had been a hot and frustrating day for him.

"People here are just as stupid as they are in Suffolk and Norfolk. I've seen pigsties at the back of these cottages but there's no pigs in them. Yet the road is swarming with pigs. I've got to make a return of the number of people here who prefer to keep a pig than have a bacon coupon. And little help I get from anyone!"

Lila sympathised and stood him a beer. "There's a train to London in half-an-hour — change at Doncaster. It's the last one."

"Then I'd better get along to the station."

Not long after he had left the *Friendship*, the phone range again. It was Ikky up at the signal box. "He's now getting on the train."

People emerged from their houses and watched the train rumble over Keadby Bridge Londonwards. They looked at one another and smiled. "Now we're got to sort 'em out."

All that evening, pigs were being herded and separated and driven home by their respective owners. Lila was given a fine leg of pork for supper and a "hand and spring" for the refrigerator. Much beer was consumed. And that was the end of the Great Keadby Pig Census. One of our trimmers, a pig-keeper himself, a sly smile on his face, jerked his thumb in the general direction of London and said: "I wonder what yon lad's got writ down."

Just as Lincolnshire lies between Norfolk and Yorkshire, so the speech of the Lincolnshire men bridges the gap between the sing-song East Anglian and blunt Yorkshire. Local people can tell in a moment from which side of the Humber a man comes as soon as he has opened his mouth.

But there is a third dialect which always intrigued me as it is different and, I suspect, more ancient than present day Yorkshire or Lincolnshire. It is the language of the waterways, the speech of the keelmen who crowd the waters of the Humber, Ouse and Trent. Their craft, bluff bowed and round sterned like an ancient Saxon keel, would come flocking out of the River Hull two hours after low water, joined by others from Salt End and Thorgumbald — sometimes fifty or sixty of them — all bound upriver with cargoes for Flixborough, Gunness, Keadby, Gainsborough and as far as Nottingham. Others branched off for the canal which led to Sheffield. Among the many other ports, towns and villages they served were Goole, York and Howdendyke.

At one time these keels (they would be called barges in the south) sailed under square sail with a square topsail set above the main. A few were sloop rigged, like the brewery keels which traded across the Humber between New Holland and Hull. Now they are all motorised. The men who manned them seemed a race apart. Most were of huge stature with great hands like plates of meat. And they could drink half-a-dozen pints of ale while I was struggling through my second. I used to meet them in the *Tiger Inn* in Hull High Street, which is quite separate from the modern town of Kingston-upon-Hull. Old Hull lay to the east of the river, which had once served as a port for the Arctic whalers before they had killed all the whales in the northern waters. There are narrow streets and musty old buildings.

The keelmen, hearty, friendly and generous, spoke a language which I found difficulty to understand at first. Shouts like ''Briggo-Oh'' (open the bridge), ''Chook a piece'' (throw a rope) and advice such as ''Thar's owt watter awa fra nesses'' (there is deep water clear of the spits). And in the pub it was a question of ''soop-oop lad'' if you got behind with your beer drinking. They were splendid folk, a chip of old England, with a wide and expert knowledge of the swift tides and constantly shifting sandbanks of the waterways which served the vast hinterland. Keelman's son married keelman's daughter, and always had done without any weakening of their mighty strain. And may it always be so!!

Martinet outward bound from London River.

CHAPTER ELEVEN

Kitty Witch of Yarmouth Town

A YARMOUTH SHANTY

The Farmer has his rent to pay
  Haul, you joskins, haul
And seed to buy, I've heard him say.
  Haul, you joskins, haul
But we who plough the North Sea deep
Though never sowing, always reap
The harvest which to all is free
And Gorleston Light is home for me
  Haul, you joskins, haul.

WHEN farm hands went to sea this was the shanty bawled at them by the regular Yarmouth fishermen of years gone by. It was written down for me by the late Ronnie Balls, who was skipper of a drifter before he was 21. The above lines were all he could recollect from the shanty his father taught him. The tune has been lost.

When harvesting on the Norfolk and Suffolk farms was finished there was little or no work for the hands so they made their way, generally on foot, over long distances, to Yarmouth quay. There they were recruited to help with the herring fishing, which started just after land harvests were in. They were by no means expert seamen but strong, useful labourers on deck when it came to hauling nets day and night. The fishermen called them ''joskins'' because they wore the soft leather leggings known by that name which were part of their customary attire on the land. So as they completed one harvest they came down to the sea to reap another — the herring harvest.

Ronnie Balls was a sterling character of the old school. He had known my mother's family in Kessingland and Kirkley when all the menfolk were away fishing most of the year, either trawling or drifting. I asked him what they were like and his brief description of them was enough. ''They were hard men, like all the others,'' he said. Ronnie had been a hard man, too, in his younger days. He had only half an ear one side. He had rushed along the deck to save a man's life as a trawl wire was about to break with the full weight of the ship and trawl on it in heavy weather. He pushed the man clear, who had not sensed the

Steel barge *Greenhithe* in the Thames.

danger. As the wire snapped and the ends whipped into the air one part caught Ronnie's ear and cut it in two. Luckily he had a clean white shirt in his kitbag, so he tied the sleeves round his head and wound the rest of it round his neck to stop the bleeding — and went on fishing!

We often broadcast together in an East Anglian programme called "Down to the Sea". It was he who told me about Kitty Witch, who lived in an ancient hovel in what became known as Kitty Witch's Row. Old Yarmouth was little more than a series of narrow passages called "rows". They were so narrow that special handcarts had to be made with the wheels underneath instead of at the sides. Many of these old cottages backed on to the medieval town wall so that the wall formed the rear of the cottage.

Kitty Witch was respected and feared. She was what would now be called a clairvoyant. After the young Ronnie Balls had "tried to blow the hell out of the North Sea" as a new skipper and twice lost all his gear, he was advised by an old man in the fishmarket to go and see Kitty Witch before he sailed again.

"I laughed at the idea. I thought he was just an ignorant old man harbouring a lot of foolish superstitions. Whatever would other skippers think of me if they found out that I had been to see Kitty Witch! I should be ridiculed. However, I had another bad voyage and a poor catch: so before leaving port again I thought no harm would be done if I crept up there after dark to hear what the old witch had to say. I knocked on her door and she called out 'Come in' and I found her sitting in a wooden arm-chair at a grubby old table. She had long grey hair and her haggard, unwashed face made her look just as you would expect a witch to look. All she needed was a tall black hat and a besom to complete the picture. Before I could tell her what I'd come for, she croaked 'You've had no luck in the fishing, young man.' I nodded. 'Then you must do what Kitty tells you and sail on the next midnight tide.' I said I would do as she said, not believing her advice, and turned to go, hoping no-one had seen me.

'Sign my book before you go' she said, calling me back from the door. She had a great thick book and opened it for me to sign, writing by my name the tide on which I was to sail. I felt a bit of a chump, but looking down the page I got the surprise of my life. There were the names of all the finest and most successful skippers who had ever sailed out of Yarmouth. They had all been to Kitty Witch!

I sailed when she said I should and never had a better haul. I could see the mass of herring shimmering as we started to get the nets in. Then a Dutch schoot came ploughing over our gear and cut the lot adrift. We lost the fish, nets and all.

Back in Yarmouth I went straight up to Kitty Witch and started to give her a piece of my mind. But she held up her hand in the middle of my remonstrances and said 'Hold you on, young feller. Don't blame poor old Kitty. Maybe you've forgot that *you never paid me.*'"

Much has been written, many photographs preserved, and many tales told of the halcyon days of the Yarmouth herring fishery. Hundreds of Scottish women came south to do the gutting and cleaning. Kippering, salting, pickling, boat repairs and net making were all part of a huge industry. Sometimes six hundred million herrings were caught between the latter end of August and Christmas. Now, at the time of writing, there is not a single drifter out of Yarmouth. The port has been taken over by the oil rig industry, apart from a few coasters bringing grain, coal, cattle-feed and chemical fertilisers.

The last time I saw the fish quay crowded with drifters was not long after the Second World War. I was in a 170 ton steel barge named the *Greenhithe*, which had been repaired after we had been machine-gunned off Kessingland. Later she was sunk in collision in the Thames at the time of the invasion of Normandy and raised again by the P.L.A. salvage vessels. She was still seaworthy even after all her misfortunes. A previous skipper George Dray had been driven ashore in her on Corton beach and once she was in collision with the *Will Everard* in a barge race when being sailed by Arthur Finch of Mistley.

We loaded cattle cake in London for Yarmouth and set off in hazy, calm weather with barely enough wind to take us out of the Thames. Then came the fog, so dense that when the mate walked forward, he disappeared. The length of the barge was 89 feet, and from aft I could not see that far. Off the Nore fog bells of ships at anchor sounded like a ghostly orchestra.

Each ebb tide we drove along, lead-line on the go and sometimes going stern first with the anchor dredging along the edge of the Maplin Sands. There was not an air of wind, and the sails hung dripping like wet washing on a housewife's line. When the tide was flowing against us the fog would lift a little to give us a brief sight of nearby buoys and seamarks, but there was no wind to sail against it. On the next ebb the fog would shut down again as thick as ever.

For four days and four nights we drifted on until we were able to hear the fog signal of Yarmouth pierheads. Once I caught a shadowy glimpse of the South Pier (Gorleston). Down went the anchor. There was not a breath of wind to sail into the harbour. We shouted and blew morse signals on our foghorn for the tug *Richard Lee Barber* to come out and tow us in. But with visibility nil her skipper refused to move.

About midday the mate heard the swash-swash of a screw. Out of the fog loomed a Peterhead drifter, very close and likely to run us down. We heard a Scottish voice call out "It's a barge" and we rang our bell furiously. We could just make out her shape though he was only a few yards away.

"What's your position?" came a voice from the drifter's bridge.

"Right off the pierheads," I answered. There was a pause as she slid by. Then:

"What pierheads?"

Later she was towed off Gorleston beach by the local lifeboat.

In the afternoon came the faintest little draught from the south-east — a fair wind into the harbour. We hastily set the topsail and staysail, hove up the anchor, and headed for the sound of the pierhead fog signal. Nearby another barge, the *Will Everard*, was doing the same. The flood tide had just begun and I steered for what I hoped was the harbour entrance. I was fearful we might collide with the *Will Everard* or get set onto the pier. I could hear the master of the *Will Everard* cursing the tug skipper for refusing to come out.

A dark shadow in the fog came and went like an optical illusion. I heard the tide round the base of the south pier. The shadow could have been the *Will Everard* but at last I saw that it was Gorleston Pier. We drove inside. I could see misty human wraiths above us and someone shouted "What barge is that?" I was too busy to answer. I heard the mate call out: "I can see the *Will* . . . close. close . . . she's head up." Our little south-easterly air was just sufficient to hold us out of the right-angled bend known as Brush Bend, from which the tide ran straight north up the long harbour. To keep clear of the other barge I had the mate touch the anchor on the bottom so that we swung stern up the harbour. Thus I could control the movement of the barge in the swift-running tide as the anchor, on a short chain, rattled along the bottom — a manoevre known as "drudging". The *Will's* topsail disappeared up-harbour and we followed steadily stern-first with the anchor still dragging the bottom to keep us out of trouble. As we proceeded up the harbour the visibility improved, the fog broken up by the buildings ashore. For over a mile we could see small ships, tugs and hundreds of drifters moored to the quays. It was the last time Yarmouth was to see so many fishermen in the port. I never saw such vast numbers again. And now there are none.

It was strange that of all the craft fog-bound in the harbour that day, the only vessels which managed to move were two old fashioned spritsail barges without any form of power or sophisticated navigational equipment.

Barge *Greenhithe* in Sea Reach, River Thames, outward bound after repairs had been made following a machine-gun strafing off Kessingland.

CHAPTER TWELVE

Wrecked On a Farmyard

JACK o' Lanterns on the marshes, the call of the curlew and the tinkle of the tides round the leeboards — that was supposed to be the romance and fascination of trading up the Essex creeks in a sailing barge years ago. But it wasn't always like that.

I remember coming up the Whitaker channel in the little old *Hambrook* (the "Hambone" they used to call her because you didn't earn enough in her to have any meat on it) over forty years ago, bound for Battlesbridge with maize from London. It was November time and "mizzly thick o' rain" as they used to say in those parts. Daylight fled us before we got to the Ridge buoy but with little paltry airs drawing out of Shore Ends, which mark the entry to the River Crouch, we kept turning away up on the flood with the mate on the lead-line — two fathoms and lee-oh — hoping to reach Burnham that night to get a loaf of bread and a pint.

Visibility was so bad that we could hardly see the bank of the river, but when we reckoned we were above the Roach it fell a fatal calm and I sent the mate forward to keep a look out for the first of the yachts, for although winter was on us there were still a tidy few out on their moorings, probably a hundred or so. I didn't want to let a loaded barge drive up athwart that lot. We would down anchor at the first sign of them and get ashore on Tom Rice's Hard. Once on the sea wall, fog or no fog, I knew the mate's long legs would outpace me to the nearest pub. He had had no beer for two days, which was a serious matter.

The mate was a stranger to the Crouch and I kept calling out to him "Can you see anything?"; and he kept saying "no", until at last he cried; "Yes, I can. I can see a flour mill." My apologies, gentlemen, but I knew what he meant. He had got a glimpse of the Royal Corinthian Yacht Club. "Let go". Down went the anchor and in a matter of minutes the mainsail was brailed up, topsail run down and clewed in, foresail and staysail stowed and the riding light up. Thirteen and a half minutes later the pints were on the counter. The first part of our journey had been successfully accomplished.

Next day we sailed up to Fambridge ("*not Fam* bridge, *Farm* bridge. Talk Essex man," old Phil Finch used to say). There we had to bring up because the wind was straight down and the channel completely blocked by yachts. Anxious to save my tide to Hullbridge, I went ashore and had a swear-off with the yacht-

Hambrook slashing into the River Colne against a strong northerly wind, carrying a deck stack of barley.

minder, threatening to get under way and batter a path through the lot if he didn't come out and shift some of them. This he refused to do, but when we got underway and started to make long and short tacks through the fleet he suddenly appeared with a motor boat and yanked the offending ones inshore. (This proves that, contrary to modern cultural thought, threats and violence often bring quicker and more definite results than sweet reasonableness and intellectual argument.)

Another difficulty over, we twizzled away up to Hullbridge, just round the bend by a farmyard, where there was a barge mooring. In accordance with the usual practice, we let go our main anchor downstream and took the mooring chain in over aft so that the barge was moored fore and aft and could not swing athwart the creek, damage herself or sit on her own anchor when the water had ebbed away.

Tides were neap and lazy, and having got thus far we had to wait a couple of days for them to swell enough to carry us right up the creek to the mill at Battlesbridge. This time could be spent pleasantly enough between pints in the pub and doing a bit of shooting and snaring to help the grub locker. Country bumpkins in the barges could almost live off what they got ashore — an old hare, a rabbit or two and perhaps a pheasant on a moonlight night — and fish they baited off the quarter boards, and save their money for beer or the old woman, according to whether they were married or single. The Cockneys and townies often used to spend all their money on beer but didn't know how to replenish the pot; so they used to moan about "starvation freights" and refused to sail until the owners sent them down more money.

Soon we had company. We saw a topsail and a staysail over the marshes bowling up the creek with a light north east wind. It was my old friend Rodney Wright in the *Pride of Ipswich*, a regular trader to Battlesbridge and part owner of his barge. He berthed alongside us and passed the opinion that we should have water up next day. In the meantime we saw the battered trilby hat and long beard of old Dicky Daniels, the huffler, coming along the south bank. He waved his walking stick (which he generally used as a mooring post for a boat's painter) and called out: "You'll have water up tomorrow but I can't come after you because I've got a Dutchman to bring down."

"Never mind, Bob", Rodney said. "I'll give you a hand up with your barge and then you can come down and lend me a hand with mine. I know this creek as well as he does."

The crews of the *Hambrook* and the *Pride of Ipswich* trod the path to *The Barge* at the head of the creek that evening, and also sampled the ale in *The Hawk* further up the road. The landlord of *The Hawk* beat us at darts and demanded a trip up the creek in the barge instead of the usual winner's beer. Next morning he turned up at Hullbridge, armed with a shopping bag full of brown ale bottles.

We passed the stern mooring over Rodney's barge, canted the *Hambrook* head up and away we went. Our worst stretch was the bit round Old Tree Point, where there was not room to wind, and Rodney stood by with a setting boom on the quarter, the mate with another boom on the lee side forward, and the landlord of *The Hawk* was at the foresail halyards to drop the headsail down if she didn't come round in time. The *Hambrook* was small, but far from handy. She had been "rose on" (made higher in the sides to carry more cargo) having originally been a little stumpy named *Morley*. As a topsail barge with a bowsprit she was a fine old box at sea and as tight as a bottle, but as stubborn as a mule in short turns up a narrow creek.

The first board on the point was a pantomime. "Down foresail" and the mate bore on his setting boom on the lee bank while Rodney shoved on his to windward aft. The landlord wasn't quick enough with the halyards so the mate left his setting boom for a second, cast the halyards off, and down clattered the foresail with the landlord buried underneath it. Round came the barge "Up foresail", and the landlord came hurtling out of the folds like a flying angel, landing with a sickening thud across the hatch coamings. "Let go yer bowline", and the mate, throwing his setting boom across the prostrate landlord, unceremoniously trod on him as he dashed to the fore shroud. No sooner had the barge gathered a little way than the foresail had to come down again and the whole operation repeated on the other bank. This time the landlord, feeling that he was in the way, retreated aft just in time to catch the pin of the mainsheet block on his knee as the mainsail slogged across the horse. He swore and called for help but Rodney, who was an old friend of his, pushed him down the cabin steps with a brief ''Get down there out the bloody way.''

Once round Old Tree Point we fetched away up to the mill and tied her up under the grain sucker. Then we went below and drank the landlord's brown ale, which was excellent, though he was too sick with pain to drink any himself. But still, he'd had his trip.

Summer had come by the time I met Rodney again in the same creek, and funnily enough the circumstances were almost the same. The ageing Dicky Daniels (he must have been well over eighty) was not well enough to huffle us up so once again Rodney stepped into the breach and up we went again, leaving the *Pride* on the mooring at Hullbridge for the next day's tide up. No sooner had we moored the *Hambrook* at the mill than there came a freak tempest, blowing like hell let loose for about half an hour. Then all was calm again. We went across to *The Barge* and settled to our beer and cheese when the mate of the *Pride* came running in, all puff and blow and sweat.

''Our barge is sunk.''

Rodney could not believe his ears. ''Sunk. What do you mean — sunk?''

''She's full of water, skipper. She dragged in that squall . . . .''

We didn't wait for any more but walked and ran as fast as we could down the creekside path until we could see the *Pride of Ipswich.* At first she looked as

Stack barges from Essex bringing hay up London River to feed the city's horse transport. They returned with horse manure for the farms.

though she was all right but the tide was ebbing fast by then and her deck was nicely clear of the water as if she was lying afloat loaded. We had some trouble reaching Rodney's boat because there was a bull among a lot of cows in the field abreast of the barge and he came running at us so that we had to retreat into the creek and throw lumps of mud at him before he would let us by.

Eventually he let us alone and we scrambled aboard. Poor Rodney was heartbroken. The water had been half way up the cabin and ruined all his and the mate's bedding and belongings. Most of the cargo (maize in the main hold and oats forward) was obviously spoiled.

We saw what had happened. The *Pride* had dragged her anchor and sat on the heap of chains and half buried anchors that formed the mooring. On the low water we found under the cabin floor a great hole scored in her bottom.

I well remember Rodney Wright's words.

"I've sailed the North Sea and Channel, winter and summer, from the Tyne to the Isle of Wight, gales, fogs, anything you like. And here I am wrecked in a bloody farmyard."

Next day we brought the *Hambrook* down and salvaged 48 quarters of dry oats out of the fore hold and took it back up to the mill. Then we came alongside her again and with the help of farm-hand labour took the wet stuff out of her, unloading it in Rotherhithe for the Dessicated Grain Company — and pooh, didn't it stink by the time we sailed up Limehouse Reach. Even the cabin lamp wouldn't burn! What happened to it? It was washed, cleaned and dried until it looked like a heap of lovely golden maize. Then it was sold for corn flakes.

That was the end of the *Pride of Ipswich* as a working barge. Someone bought her as a yacht and put great diesel motors in her with some idea of sailing to South Africa. But several years later I saw her serving as a houseboat in the inner harbour at Ramsgate. Rodney's dead now, and the *Hambrook* became a houseboat at Woolverstone up the River Orwell.

You didn't have to sail the broad oceans for excitement and adventure. You could get plenty of it up an Essex creek. The ancient and picturesque cottages by the salt marshes and creeks of the low-lying Essex coast, now eagerly sought after at fancy prices by London week-enders, were very far from popular in the days of our great-grandfathers. Especially were they the dread of womenfolk enticed there from the uplands, as natives called the rising ground between Colchester, Witham, Chelmsford and Romford; roughly the track of the present A.12 motor road.

Down on those marshlands lived a hardy race of men, nearly all fishermen, bargemen and wildfowlers. Their home was the mudflat, their living, the tidal creek. They were known in Essex as "The Peculiar People." Tales were told of their being web-footed and I have myself seen them run across soft mud without sinking in. If it was especially slimy they strapped things called "splatchers"

St Peter's-on-the-Wall. At one time it had three short towers and the marks of their foundations can still be seen. Essex farmers once used it as a barn until the Diocese of Chelmsford restored it to its proper use.

to their feet, like miniature skis, and slithered across to retrieve wild fowl they had shot or to tend their creek nets.

For the men, always outdoors, it was a vigorous and healthy world; but for the women in the cottages it spelt nothing but sickness and death. Damp, marsh fever, cold mists and utter loneliness took fearful toll of them and it is said that few lived into their thirties, by which time their poor corpses were laid in a punt and ferried up to the nearest churchyard. Then off would go the husband to the "upland" to get another wife. Having courted and won her he would bring her back to the marshlands, where, after perhaps bearing one or two children, she would wither and die like the others. Then back to the uplands he would have to go to get another. Many of the marshmen had as many as a dozen wives — in succession, of course; nothing immoral about these chaps — and I was told (though I do not believe it) that a farmer at Benfleet had twenty five wives in all and his son, by the time he was thirty five, had had fourteen.

Even as far back as 1722, when Daniel Defoe (the author of *Robinson Crusoe*) made his tour of the Eastern Counties, this observant gentleman remarked in his notes " . . . when they took the young lasses out of the wholesome fresh air (from the uplands, that is) they were healthy, fresh and clear, and well, but when they came out of their native air into the marshes, among fogs and damps, there they presently changed their complexions, got an ague or two, and seldom held it above half a year, a year at the most." So off to the uplands for a fresh 'un.

Not long before the last war I landed at Foulness Island (at the entrance to the River Crouch) in company with the late Archie White, the Essex artist. The

97

population was sparse and they lived just as their ancestors had done. There were no roads, no post, no medical facilities of any sort. I remember Archie asking a leathery looking individual who gave us a pint of home-brewed beer, "But what do you do if you want a doctor?"

The marshman smiled and shrugged his shoulders. "We just dies of ourselves," he said.

North East Essex still retains some of its old rural life and character, closely allied to that of neighbouring Suffolk. Wildfowling, fishing and barging were common interests on either side of the River Stour, which has formed a natural boundary between the two "peoples" for well over a thousand years. The difference between them is still evident, but was much more pronounced thirty or forty years ago. We have to remember that fundamentally the Suffolker is an Anglian, tall, rangy and possessed of a casual nature born of supreme self-confidence. The Essexman is a Saxon (an "East Saxon") — shorter, broad-shouldered, stubborn and shrewd.

My old friend and skipper, the late Percy Quantrill, Suffolk born and bred, was once asked by a stranger visiting Pin Mill how to get to Harwich. After explaining the devious route round the lanes which encompass Holbrook, Harkstead and Erwarton, Percy said: "And when you get into Essex you turn hard a-port (sharp left, to you) and you'll hit the Harwich Road."

"But how shall I know when I am in Essex?" the stranger asked.

Percy scratched his head. "Well, you see a lot of Essexmen about." Shiremen might laugh at this, but Percy was quite serious. The racial difference in the two populations was quite obvious to him. If in those days you stood Ephraim Sharman (Pin Mill) alongside Frank Shuttlewood (Paglesham) you would have a prime example of the Angle and the Saxon.

The only people imposed upon these original Anglo-Saxon elements were French Huguenots and the earlier Flemish weavers brought over by King Edward the Third to establish the weaving trade in Eastern England. Many settled in the small towns and villages on the North bank of the River Blackwater, which the East Saxons used to call the Pant. On Mersea Island there lived a splendid old character by the name of Bill Wyatt, a very English Englishman. He regarded with scorn the descendants' Huguenot names such as Musset and De Witt, who to this day occupy much of the island. "They ain't English," he would say "they come over with the Hottentots."

Out of this grew an Essex tale which few outside the area could properly appreciate. There is a place on the south bank of the Blackwater estuary called Bradwell-next-Sea (to distinguish it from the other Bradwells) and here was an old Roman fort and settlement called Othona. There are still some boats called *Othona* belonging to that part of the marshy coastline. It was built to keep rampaging Saxons out but eventually they overran it and, as the Romans withdrew, made a fortified village of Othona and called it in their own language

Ithanchester. They were pagans until a famous Saxon bishop named Cedd (later Saint Cedd) came along to convert the wild adventurers to Christianity. Under his supervision the old Roman wall was dismantled to provide building materials for a church. That was in 600 A.D. And there it stands to this very day, probably the oldest building in England, having weathered 1400 years of North Sea storms and tidal floods. Many a Norman and Medieval church has crumbled and fallen into ruin in much less time. Having completed his church, called St Peter's-on-the-Wall, St Cedd looked across the river and saw Mersea Island.

"Now," he said, "I will carry the word of God to whoever lives over there."

So they provided the good man with a boat and oars and he rowed across the water and landed on what is now Mersea Hard. Stepping ashore he saw a fisherman in cloth cap and blue jersey. (They used to say Mersea fishermen wore five jerseys and took two off in the summer.) St Cedd hailed him.

"I am Bishop Cedd and I have converted the people of Ithanchester to Christianity and helped them to build the church of St Peter you can see across there. What do you call this place?"

"Mersea."

"Do you know Jesus Christ here?"

The fisherman shook his head.

"No, no. All Wyatts, Witts and Mussets here."

Inside the old Saxon Chapel of St Peter's-in-the-Wall at Bradwell-next-Sea, Essex.

99

CHAPTER THIRTEEN

Ice Floes in the Thames Estuary

A MAN on ice-watch in the weather rigging, beating his one free hand against a snow-covered monkey-jacket in a vain effort to retain some bodily warmth; the mate forrard fending off heavy lumps of drifting ice; the helmsman (myself) stamping numbed feet in the open fronted wheelhouse. Away to starboard a huge ice-floe, three miles long, grumbled slowly eastward on the ebb tide. And all the time there was the grinding, crashing noise of ice against our wooden hull. Who would have thought that these conditions were being faced by the 59-year-old barge *Cambria* in the Thames Estuary. The whole scene, the intense cold, the flurries of snow and the clatter of pack-ice, was more like Antarctica. I had never seen anything like it in British Home Waters. It was January 1963, the start of a memorable year, and the big freeze-up went on for 70 days — December 26th to March 6th. Parts of the Thames were frozen over and the Medway was solid ice. Kentishmen could walk across their river at Gillingham.

Nothing like it had been seen since the Great Frost of January 31st 1814, when Londoners held a fair on the Thames. On that occasion they actually had a bonfire on the ice in the middle of the river, with people skating round it and chaps with hand carts selling hot roasted potatoes. Entertainment stalls and tents were set up and the merrymaking on ice went on for five days. The thaw set in on February 5th when there was a shift of wind to the south and rain. The ice had built up into great humps because the archways of old London Bridge were too narrow to allow passage for the floes coming down from up-river. When these huge lumps of ice broke loose in the thaw they went crashing down the river doing untold damage to wharves and moored vessels and causing several people to lose their lives.

We sailed up London River after a bitter Christmas passage from Yarmouth during which we had fearsome snow squalls from the east. We ran the barge in shallow water whenever we could to keep out of the big ship channels. Sometimes we had been snow blinded for long periods and had to rely on the lead-line and compass. Sea water froze in the scuppers.

On January 1st we entered the Surrey Commercial Dock and under topsail berthed alongside a French ship, named the *Vercors*, in the Canada Yard, to load for Yarmouth. Her crew were Bretons and the mate invited us aboard to take wine. "We are British, the same as you," he said. They were over generous

River Medway frozen over in 1814.

with the red wine and we both suffered stomach pains and vomiting after getting back aboard the *Cambria*.

We were a long time loading our one hundred tons of ground nut extract (cattle feed). The dockers were forever belly-aching for extra money — snow money — ice money — cold weather money — backing their various claims with the oft repeated phrase "It's the conditions we're working under". No one mentioned the fact that we were going to sea under these wintry conditions. No long tea breaks, dinner time booze or nipping out to the betting shops for us. And no home and fireside for us in the evening. I told one of them this and he said "Well, that's your pigeon. It's yer job, ain't it." Dockers and sailormen rarely saw eye to eye. But it must be said that a docker's one saving grace (on good days only) was his sense of humour.

On the tenth day we scrambled out of the dock into Limehouse Reach, heaving on a dolly-wire, shoving on hitchers and setting a bit of sail when there was a clear eye through the mass of abandoned lighters. Modern lightermen are not always in constant attendance on their lighters, especially in such vile freezing weather with the east wind nipping through your bones however many jerseys and pairs of trousers you wore.

It was a dead beat to windward down London River and late that day we rounded to a heavy mooring buoy off Greenhithe. Covered with thick ice and snow, the *Cambria* looked like a Polar expedition ship. We robbed every coal barge we could get near and after dark some of the firm's office coal disappeared into our lockers. I told the yard foreman about it a few days later but he turned his back and walked away as though he hadn't heard what I said. His father had been a bargeman! For fourteen days we hung on to that mooring buoy, covered with snow and ice, which we attempted to shovel off the decks morning and evening, as well as knocking it out of the rigging. All the time the easterly gale blew and there was not a hope of getting away to sea. We had so many wires and ropes on the buoy that our moorings looked like a spiders web. Luckily it was a buoy laid specially for big ships.

At last the wind shifted to the north and the snow storms eased off. Determined to get on with the voyage at any opportunity we set all plain sail and anchored for the night in the Lower Hope. There was still a lot of ice coming down the river and we wondered what conditions were like further down in the Estuary. The next day the wind edged more to the north-west and as we were preparing to get underway the motor barge *Hydrogen* came up on the last of the flood and passed quite close. Her skipper, Charlie Crix, was an old friend and a seaman of great experience, so I sung out to him: "What's it like below?"

"Don't you go any further today" he shouted. "We've been frozen in at the South-East Maplin for a day and a night. You'll never get through under sail." In his youth he had been whaling in the Antarctic so he knew what he was talking about.

So another day and a night went by. I was on deck before day light, awakened by the drip of melting ice from our rigging. The wind was south-west. Away we went, full of hope, squared off to a fair wind of only moderate strength. The hills of Kent to the southward were an unbroken white and to port we saw fishing boats frozen tight in Hole Haven Creek. But surely, I thought, a south west wind should start a general thaw.

We reached the South East Maplin buoy and I saw that Charlie Crix had been right. I measured the great ice floe to starboard with an old sextant I had saved from my ocean voyaging. It was exactly 3¼ miles long, and was proceeding slowly down past the Nore on the ebb tide. Everywhere there were ice floes, big and small, and Vernon Parker, the mate, stood in the bows thrusting them aside with a long hitcher, like a harpooner. Up in the main ratlines the third hand, John Dickens, kept a look-out for thin patches and directed me accordingly. More and heavier ice-packs came at us as the flood tide started and there were times when, even with our fair wind, the barge slowed almost to a stop. I dreaded being completely ice-bound out here in the Estuary and perhaps having our barge crushed under us. There would be no chance of help. No ships were moving.

As we crept slowly to the Wallet Spitway, where there is a passage over the sands, the tide was just right for us to cross over. In the distance, nearer the Essex shore, there seemed to be less ice. With both Parker and Dickens in the rigging we put her to it and crashed into the pack covering the shallow water. The *Cambria* started to slow up. Both lads came down and jabbed and beat at the ice with anything they could lay their hands on. "She's still going ahead" they called back, but just as we were nearly over she all but stopped. I jabbed over the quarters with a boat oar and hove the leeboards up and down to try to disturb the more solid packs of ice. We were making about half a knot. Then came a smart puff of wind and the two lads managed to crack a heavy piece lying across our bows. *Cambria* moved again — and we were over in the deep water of the Wallet channel. Breasting the flood we headed for Harwich in fairly clear water. We would go in there for the night.

Looking astern I saw an amazing sight. A huge floe had come out of the River Crouch and fast in it were two yachts, some dinghies and one of the fairway buoys — a complete river scene in ice.

By the time we reached the approaches to Harwich the tide was done and the ebb was running out of the harbour. We ran into a wall of ice and in spite of the fact that we had a fair wind into the harbour, the *Cambria* came to a grinding halt. She could go no further and as soon as the way was off her we were frozen in fore and aft. We could see into the harbour. Fed up, cold and hungry, we stowed the sails as best we could. The brails made the canvas crackle like splintering wood. We let go the anchor with a run and it came to rest on top of the ice. We hove it up again and hammered a hole for it to drop in. We let go a second time and it disappeared. When we had paid out thirty five fathoms of chain the ice closed over it. I only hoped that this would hold the ice floe as well as the barge. There was a risk that we might be carried off towards the Cork Sand — ice floe, barge and all.

Cold weather for bargemen.

It got dark early. John got a roaring fire going in the cabin and Vernon stoked up another in the forecastle. Pints of hot tea, bowls of hot stew — and we rolled into our bunks, too tired to worry any more.

I awoke with a start about four o'clock in the morning and scampered up the companion, wondering where we were. We were in the same place, but still wedged in the ice. I lay on the cabin locker, stoked the fire up, and waited for the dawn. I must have dozed because it was broad daylight when I woke up. I immediately went on deck, and to my surprise the ice had gone and we lay in clear water. I could see our ice floe to seaward. I called the lads and in quick time the anchor was up, sails set and the barge chuckling along through Harwich Harbour and up the River Orwell to Pin Mill, where I lived. Along the shores it was pitiful to see the swans and coots frozen to death between lumps of ice. We got the boat in the water and with some difficulty battered our way to the Hard. We managed to free one swan which showed signs of life but he keeled over and died when we got him ashore. He was starved as well as frozen.

It was now January 27th. Four weeks had gone by since we went up to the dock to load, and still we had not reached our destination. The wind shifted into the east again and although the river anchorage kept clear of serious floes, the ice and snow covering the mud flats did not start to melt for another week.

And so to Yarmouth with a north west breeze, arriving there on February 3rd and discharging our cargo the next day.

We had taken five weeks to load, make the passage, and discharge. We sailed ''by the share'', and on this freight our share was well in the red. The only consolation we got was that although we had taken five weeks, a motor barge which loaded at the same time for the same place did not arrive in Yarmouth until a fortnight after the *Cambria*; so she had taken seven weeks!

There was no money in barging that winter. Many laid their barges up and went home: and come the spring they were just as well off as us!!

Berthed on the London River.

CHAPTER FOURTEEN

Dock Life in London

IN THE wake of the Great Freeze of 1963 came a spell of stormy weather. Strong winds from the north and north-east gave us little rest. On top of that, work for the *Cambria* was hard to come by and it was not until February 20th that we were fixed to load bales of pulp for Dover. It was only the second freight of the year. There were several motor barges loading ahead of us and we were last under the crane.

They were big bulky bales and the 80 tons we were chartered to carry nearly filled the hold. I was told that this pulp was for making five pound notes, but there were not many five pound notes in it for us. To make a profitable job of it we had to do it quickly. Luck was not with us. A drifting, unmanned, lighter in the dock crashed our bulwarks down and we had to stop at the Greenhithe yards for repairs. The shipwrights did well to get things put right in three days and we slammed away down to the open waters of the Estuary against a strong north-east wind. We lowered our 38 foot bowsprit down and set a medium sized jib which had seen better days. Being "light on" with plenty of freeboard, the *Cambria* breasted the seas off the North Foreland and I told the mate: "If that old jib hangs on long enough for us to get an offing from that surf battering the chalk cliffs, we can bear up through the Downs for Dover." Until we got that offing the barge had to put up with a hammering from the north-easterly seas. Gradually we drew out from the land, nearly as far as Broadstairs Knoll, when all of a sudden, in a matter of seconds, the jib blew to pieces, parts of it flying away in the breeze. "Jib's gone", the mate shouted, a little alarmed by the sight and sound of the swell thundering on the steep-to shore. But we were far enough to up-helm and free the mainsheet. The third hand ran to help me get the wheel over and the *Cambria* sped away like a train for the South Foreland and Dover.

By noon we were in the harbour and next day discharged our bales. None of the motor barges had arrived, they having gone into the Medway for shelter. Before any of them arrived we were on our way back to London to load 100 tons of maize meal for Yarmouth. For a sailing barge work was so scarce that we rarely got a full freight. We could carry 170 tons. The pulp freight to Dover left us £37 14s 8d to share between the three of us, but the two youngsters stuck it well and took the rough with the smooth. They had a "ship-pride" all too

A London docker, assisted by two of *Cambria's* crew.

rare in modern times. It was the first money we had earned since the disastrous freeze-up freight which had ended only three weeks earlier.

It was while we were loading the pulp out of the *Fidra*, which was a Swedish ship, that I made friends with one of the mates by the name of Erikson. He claimed to be the nephew of the famous Erikson of Mariehamn who owned and operated the last of the big four-masters bringing grain from Australia round Cape Horn. This *Fidra* mate was a native of the Aaland Islands in Finland, the home of many fine sailing ship men — most of them of Swedish descent.

''Then you are a Swedish Finn'', I said, when we were having a pint in the *Tooks Arms* in Glengall Road, outside the Millwall Dock. With typical Scandinavian humour, he shook his head and gave a wry smile.

''No, I am a Finnish Swede.''

He told me how he had fought against the Russian Army in the Russo-Finnish War of 1939-40.

''I am a sailor, so they make me a soldier in the artillery. We have not much shells and bullets and the Russians are many. We stop them under General Mannheim. I have two guns. Phut! one I fire. Other one tomorrow.''

It was a gallant stand against overwhelming odds.

''What did you think of the Russian Army?''

He did not reply; just spit on the floor.

One day he urged me to visit him in his luxurious flat in Stockholm. I asked him how I should find him, as I spoke no Swedish and had never been to Stockholm.

106

"Very easy you find me." he said, "In Stockholm there is a big square. You stand in the middle of the square and shout loud 'Where dat bastard Erikson' . . . and dey will show you where I live."

In spite of such detailed instructions, I never got there!

Swedish seamen always congregated in the *Took's Arms*, just as the "Norskies" (Norwegians) could be found in the *Blue Post* outside the West India Dock Gate, Cockney Watermen in the *Oporto* and the *Eastern*, and dockers in the *Star of the East*. In the *Railway*, which was known the world over as *Charlie Brown's*, you could find every race, colour and creed under the sun. There was hardly ever any trouble or violence in these dockland pubs in spite of the mixture of the races forming the clientelle. It was far more peaceful, and certainly more friendly, than London's West End.

The Chinese of Pennyfields (which was known among genuine East-enders as "The Causeway") provided excellent eating places. In fact no West End gourmet ever tasted such good Chinese food as that which was obtainable around the Pennyfields area. We ate where the Chinese ate, and they would not have put up with what they called "English Chinese food." One elderly Chinese ran a restaurant in a bomb-damaged house. He told us that to appreciate real Chinese food it must be eaten as soon as it is cooked. He would ask us what time we wanted our meal and we would go across the road and have a couple of pints while he got it ready. I have been in many Chinese restaurants since but never had food so appetising as that old man dished up. "You say 9 o'clock and it will be ready at 9 o'clock and you must eat it then." He got two cooks to come from China, but they would first write back to ask if he had a television set in the kitchen. "So I buy a television and then I get the best cooks in China." He has gone now. I don't think his kitchen satisfied the local Council officials. But his food satisfied everyone else.

West India Dock always had a character very different from other dock areas. Nearly all the dockers were natives of the Isle of Dogs. In fact, I was told that at one time you would not get a job in "the West" if you did not live on the Isle of Dogs. Most of them had lived there for generations. They looked alike, were much the same height, and, of course, swore they were not related. To we "sailormen", as everyone called barge crews, they were the best dockers in London. They would stow cargoes well, work hard, help each other, and keep up a quick witted banter all day long. They had a working language of their own — "two long arms in the cupboard and a soldier" meant two bags to be stowed high under the deck and the odd space filled by shoving in one bag upright. Their humour was vulgar and the constant leg-pulling hilarious. I once took my small daughter Anne aboard the *Cambria* while we were loading cartons of fruit juice out of a ship from Israel at "O" Shed in the West India Dock. As soon as the dockers saw her coming aboard the cry went round: "Stand-by to repel boarders." This meant, among themselves, no bad language. And for the whole day there was not a swear word to be heard. Little Anne, somewhat bewildered, was continually consulted as to the best way to stow the cargo. ''Is that all right, Anne?'' and ''Anne says that set's got to go under the deck.'' And when the crane driver made a bad landing in a hold, which would normally have evoked a stream of abuse, there was not a word out of place. ''Did you see that, Anne? Oh, dear me. What a naughty crane-man. Nearly killed poor Charlie, he did.''

It was better than any music-hall entertainment.

Bad stowage of Cornish clay. Such careless work could endanger a ship in bad weather. Complaints by masters and mates were ignored at all levels.

CHAPTER FIFTEEN

Maldon's Hero

THERE is no man in the world more proud than the one who can stand at the wheel of his own ship, look up at his sails and say: "This is my all." I was fortunate enough to be able to do that after sailing the *Cambria* for twelve years under the Everard flag. I had been in the company for many years as master of the 210 ton "boomie" barge *Martinet*, the 170 ton *Greenhithe* and the 170 ton *Cambria*. I had also been fortunate in that the Everard family had always been "barge minded." They had built them, sailed them and operated them all their lives. Fred Everard and William Everard, after serving an apprenticeship as shipwrights at Fellows Yard in Great Yarmouth, had themselves built the *Cambria* and the *Hibernia*. They were handsome sister-ships and seen at sea it was almost impossible to tell one from the other. William built the *Cambria* and Fred the *Hibernia*. They were launched in 1906 and were the "Queens" of the coast.

The *Hibernia* was lost when driven ashore at Cromer in a fierce north easterly gale while under the command of Skipper Couchman. The crew were rescued by the Sheringham lifeboatmen, but the following day there was nothing of her left to be seen. It was a bitter blow to "Uncle Fred," as we used to call him. He was proud of his *Hibernia*, and good reason to be for she was, like her sister, as beautiful a barge as ever went coasting under sail.

William Everard, for as long as he lived, always kept an interest in his *Cambria*. If she needed anything I had only to ask him. As a result she was maintained in "better nick" than the average barge of her years. She was built double planked and then in her later years was doubled over again so that she was in effect treble sided. Instead of her pitch pine planking being rabbetted as was the custom in other barges, William had built her with each plank completely overlapping half of the next.

There came a time when, among a large and expanding fleet of modern motorships, the *Cambria* was a bit of a problem economically but I kept her making regular voyages between London River, Ipswich, Great Yarmouth, Wells, and often north to the Humber and Trent. We earned a fair living which was more than could be said of other sailing barges where the crews pleaded for engines or packed up altogether. The old breed of skippers were dying out. Youngsters came along, enthusiastic and hard working, but without the

109

experience of the generations before and few to teach them. Some of their craft were sold off cheaply as yachts, but they were not ''real barges'' any more, and became summer holiday vessels, with chipboard cabins and bathrooms in the hold: even pianos!

Circumstances were such that the *Cambria* remained the only working barge and I was able to keep her ploughing a lone furrow in her traditional trade. Winter and Summer, dark and daylight, she did not fail either her crew, the merchants who trusted us with valuable cargoes, or the brokers who kept faith in us. Apart from Everards, people in the London shipping business like Tom Blackburn, Raymond Sully, Maurice Gill and Bill Scholley treated the *Cambria* as they would treat any other ship; and not as an obsolete old craft run by a romantic lunatic who was trying to keep pace under sail with power driven vessels. But keep pace we did, and occasionally beat them for turn to discharge, taking short cuts across the low-ways of off-shore shoals and luffing into ports while they waited for a pilot.

I was lucky to have mates who always tried their level best, whether experienced or not, and their efforts helped me to keep the *Cambria* going as a commercial vessel. Phillip Latham, once junior clerk in an insurance office and without any seafaring background, forced himself to overcome all his failings and eventually became master of a smart little coaster. When he first joined me in the Albert Dock he could not climb more than three or four ratlines up the main rigging. Before he left he had conquered the 49 foot mainmast and could then shin on up the 43 foot topmast above it to put on a fresh truck and a new flag. There was little Peter Frost, almost straight from school; he became a coasting master, too, and met a tragic death aboard his ship in Southern Ireland. He would not stay at school because, ''The master knew nothing about winds

Cambria in a hurry, sailing up Maldon creek with the bowsprit jib set to save her tide on the mill berth.

and tides and sailing barges. I can't understand how he ever became a schoolmaster. He kept me in school late once because when he said sailing ships could only go before the wind and I had said 'Ha-ha.' Very ignorant, he was.''

Peter was a good little third hand and an excellent waterman. He had been sailing small boats single handed since he was eight years old. Vernon Parker from Colchester became a fishing skipper and Dick Durham, the last of them all, helped me with his unfailing wit and good humour as well as his untiring physical efforts. It is pleasant for me in my old age to have them write or come and visit me to reminisce and tell me their own tales of the sea. They talked sea sense, because, like me, they went to sea for a living.

As the years went by the *Cambria*'s voyages became shorter with the changing pattern of trade. The small local gas works to which we used to take coal from the Humber were shut down in a government scheme for centralisation. We ceased to unload the black diamonds from the north in such places as Harwich, Margate, Colchester and Sittingbourne. It was Plate wheat for Maldon, soya bean meal for Colchester, wheat for Ipswich, wheat for Whitstable, pea-beans for Sittingbourne, bone meal for Mistley, wheat for Rochford, fish meal, dried peas, dried blood, cartons of fruit juice, Army ammunition, bulk maize, talc, and every sort of cattle cake. We did, however, slip in a number of freights to Lowestoft, Yarmouth and Norwich.

Every sea-going barge has to pass a strict survey every four years to retain her load-line (Plimsoll Mark). If her condition does not satisfy the Board of Trade she is restricted to the smooth waters of the Thames Estuary and sheltered rivers. It was an anxious week for me as the chief London surveyor came to see her on the blocks at Pin Mill, poking, prodding and measuring for faults and weaknesses. A black shadow hung over me in case he should find something seriously wrong with her which would let me in for a repair bill amounting, perhaps, to thousands of pounds. My shipwright was the late Ted Webb of Pin Mill, probably the best barge-wright outside the London area. There was nothing he could not do in a barge, and he achieved some magnificent work on barges at various times with the absolute minimum of equipment. He walked round the *Cambria* with the surveyor, ready to make a note of any repairs or alterations demanded. Unable to stand the strain, I retired to the *Butt and Oyster* and watched them out of the window.

Presently the Surveyor came in for his lunch. I tried to be pleasant, but my heart sank when he said: ''There's one thing you must get done.'' He left me on the edge of a nervous breakdown before he added: ''Your sidelight boards are two degrees out of true. Will you tell your shipwright to weld the stanchion irons where they are worn.''

''Certainly. Anything else?''

''No, she's in good condition. I will send your new load-line certificate down from my London office.''

I tried to look unconcerned, thanked him, and refrained from kissing him on both cheeks. Light-board stanchions? Four or five pounds would cover that, and we were O.K. for another four years. Everard's didn't build tender barges, thank God. In triumph, I made a round of London brokers and secured a cargo of 150 tons of wheat, ex- s.s. *Kimbrook*, from Victoria Dock to Maldon. It is a muddy creek, somewhat cluttered up with yachts and yacht barges, with a fine old Town Quay which is always fully occupied with craft owned by people who do not go to sea for a living. We shook many of them by rattling up the narrow channel with all sail set and the bowsprit jib on her. "Never been done before" the wiseacres said, but someone managed to take a photograph. The manager of the mill situated at the top of the creek was well pleased with our prompt delivery and chartered us for his next cargo from London.

Maldon was never a progressive port and seems content these days to wallow in its charm and history. I always had the impression that the creek smelt of silt and dry rot, but the town is one of the most attractive in Essex. From its days as an ancient Celtic settlement, it came to fame in Saxon times. The East Saxons had a leader by the name of Byrhtnoth, a descendant of the Royal Saxon line and a wise ruler. He was a huge man, reputed to be seven feet in height and well versed in the strategy of warfare. An army of Vikings came sailing up the Pant (as the River Blackwater used to be called) and, landing on Northey Island, demanded gifts and gold, the Danegeld submitted to by the policy of King Ethelred the Unrede — not "unready" as has been misquoted. Rede meant wisdom and good advice but he would accept none and preferred to pay up rather than fight. Not so the mighty Byrhtnoth, who had for long diasgreed with his King over this matter. He mustered every able-bodied man in Maldon and marched them out of the town to the field opposite the "Hard" which still serves as a low-water crossing to Northey Island. In the ensuing battle the men of Maldon, greatly outnumbered, put up a heroic fight. Byrhtnoth was cut down in the thickest of the fight and "hewed", so the old poem says, and his head hacked off. His Maldon companions refused to flee and fought to the death in a corpse-ring around him. A few allies from the Midlands had fled.

Little did they know that they were fighting against one of the most famous generals of Scandanavia, Olaf Trygvasson who had already captured and sacked Ipswich. His army was composed of well trained and experienced warriors. The men of Maldon were mostly town lads who had to be shown by Byrhtnoth how to hold their shields and weapons as they lined up for the fight. But they were fighting for their homes and families and desperate courage was not lacking. They were overwhelmed and the invaders captured the town, but the fight put up by the men of Maldon has never been forgotten.

The poem "Song of Maldon", written shortly after, is probably the oldest English poem in existence. Every Essexman should read it at least six times and go and stand, as I have done, on the very field of battle and picture it all in his mind's eye. Then he will be proud to be called an Essexman. There is a statue of the bold Bryhtnoth in a niche on the outer wall of the Parish Church. It is quite inadequate for so heroic a figure. He should dominate the town as King Alfred does in Winchester

Perhaps Maldon would have become a thriving port had the builders of the canal from Chelmsford been allowed to bring it into the town, as was intended. But there seems to have been a reluctance on the part of Maldon's ruling elders to allow the town to develop into a commercially important centre of North Sea Trade. So the canal diggers had to break out to the river further downstream, at Heybridge. Thus the whole conception of future trade was frustrated and Maldon sank back into its charming lethargy.

Cambria discharging at Maldon. In the foreground is a yacht barge, *Thalatta*.

CHAPTER SIXTEEN

Chris Chataway Comes Aboard

I SAILED from Greenhithe in the *Cambria* one morning in 1955 with the strangest crew a barge could have.

First aboard, as we lay at anchor close to the *Worcester* Training Ship, was Chris Chataway, the famous athlete who was at that time preparing to run for Britain in the Olympic Games. He was something of a hero of mine, having myself been slightly athletic in my younger days. I remember the great day he ran against the almost unbeatable Czech Zatopec. I was ashore that evening in Snape, my barge having arrived at the Maltings there with a cargo of barley. I was invited to the village club social and supper. In the middle of the proceedings the chairman called for silence. ''I have an announcement to make. News has just come through . . . Chataway has beaten Zatopec.'' These last words were shouted.

A tremendous cheer went up and every villager rose to his feet and stamped and clapped for several minutes. I joined in. And here was the great Chataway himself, stepping aboard my old barge. Red haired, good looking and every inch an athlete, he shook me warmly by the hand and ''hoped he wouldn't be in the way.''

He was followed by the B.B.C. producer Richard Cawston who had planned a television programme to be called ''Away from it All''. He had researchers out all over Britain looking for people who led a simple life, unhindered by the ''rat race'' of the big cities, without the pettiness of suburbia, the noise and the traffic, and without the generally accepted shackles of convention. Chataway was to be the star of the show, interviewing such folk as a lonely wildfowler of the Essex marshes, a Scottish shepherd and myself.

Richard Cawston, who was destined to rise to great heights in the B.B.C., was unable to make the trip himself. He sent a man named Stephen Hearst, an Austrian by origin. Although it seemed strange to have a man from a land-locked country to direct a sea-faring programme, he was most co-operative and helpful in every way, shepherding his flock of cameramen, engineers and ''continuity'' people in a way that served his purpose and interfered as little as possible with the operation of sailing the barge. A most business-like chap and excellent company.

Cambria's mainsheet, block and iron traveller which thundered across the main horse when the barge tacked or gybed.

The chief cameramen was Charles de Jaegar, who had been brought from some luxurious hotel in the Middle East, where he had been filming, to sleep in our slightly damp and primitive spare bunk where, being a big man, his feet overlapped the end and rested on the edge of the gash bucket. He sighed, but did not grumble — openly. He had a clumsy looking top-heavy contraption called a ''sound-vision'' camera, mounted on a tripod. His assistant, a cheerful youngster named Johnny Ray, operated a hand-held cine-camera. He could only take silent film, whereas de Jaegar's instrument recorded both sound and vision at the same time. It was a new and very costly piece of equipment and was treated with great tenderness and reverence by everyone. Little did they know what was to happen to it.

This film trip was doomed to a series of minor disasters, starting with the announcement by a secretary-lady that she had arranged for us to all dine at the *Three Cups Inn* in Harwich at 6 pm that day. The wind was freshening from the north-east and any hope of getting to Harwich that day was out of the question.

''But it's only 50 miles,'' she said, not realising that although the passage could be made in nine or ten hours with a fair wind, it could be nine or ten *days* against a north-easter.

At last all was ready and two B.B.C. engineers asked permission to make use of my cabin. They had brought aboard a number of heavy duty batteries and some arc-lights.

The weather was not really fit to start, but with all these people agog with the excitement of the adventure, I felt I must make some show of willingness. The mate and I hove the anchor up, got the canvas on her and hauled the *Cambria* to windward down Fiddler's Reach. We knew they were going to get a bit of a shock when we opened up Sea Reach, but they were all busy to start filming.

Minor disaster No. 1 came early. The mate discovered that the mass of batteries in my cabin had been placed on the table and the seat-benches and in a hard puff were within an ace of being shot across the cabin floor as the barge heeled sharply. With the assistance of the mate they were all put down on the cabin floor and wedged in tight. This upset the wiring and when de Jaegar reported that he had no power for his sound-vision camera, the engineers came on deck and said: "We've got problems." The acting-producer, Stephen Hearst, bolted up and down the companion ladder, checking this and that and became intermediary between the engineers and the cameramen. At last, all was well and de Jaegar got his sound-vision contraption in position on the after deck, with Chris Chataway seated on the main horse with a background of wind-swelled red canvas. Just as he started to say his piece a Norwegian steamer came ploughing up Sea Reach and we were forced to tack. This was a revelation to all of them. The sails thundered, the main-sheet block started to flog and the great iron traveller to which the heavy block is hooked commenced to bang its way across the mainhorse. I yelled to Chataway to get his ass off the horse and he jumped clear. As she filled away on the new tack and all was quiet again the film crew obviously thought that such an operation could not occur again. But with heavy traffic on the river and a freshening wind as we drew away from the shelter of the land, a number of tacks were necessary. Alas, several people now sat on the main horse, discussing scripts and getting ready for the next shot. I shouted "Lee-oh" to the mate but that meant nothing to our B.B.C. friends and only at the last minute did Stephen Hearst save them from getting serious injuries from the flogging traveller. He soon sized up the situation and issued an edict: "When Bob shouts 'Lee-oh' — up asses."

Now came disasters numbers 2 and 3. For a short time we had been able to sail under the lee of the Essex shore by Shellhaven, but as we opened up the low land around Hole Haven and Canvey Island the wind headed us in a more easterly direction, a squall coming up Sea Reach with considerable weight. "Lee-oh — up asses" — and as we came head to wind, Charles de Jaegar was peering into his sound-vision thing, blissfully unaware of what was going to happen to him. Round came the barge and over she heeled at what seemed to them an alarming angle. The star camera man shot stern first into the mizzen rigging, the heavy sound-vision box and tripod on top of him. The mate rushed to save him from going over the side, hastily heaving the equipment off him. It fell on deck with a resounding thump. The engineers rushed up on deck yelling that there was a fire in the cabin. The batteries had shorted. The mate nipped down and beat it out with his cap, tearing the complicated wiring from the terminals. On deck, de Jaegar retrieved his sound-vision box. The tripod had buckled. When the batteries were once more properly connected he tried his valuable equipment, Johnny Ray and the mate holding it up for him. After a few attempts at filming, he gave it up and announced to Stephen Hearst: "You can have sound and no vision, or vision and no sound." The costly sound-vision invention had failed to stand up to the rigours of barging.

The weather was now deteriorating and I advised the film crew that we should have to anchor at Southend and await more favourable conditions. This we did. It was then agreed that the mate should scull Hearst ashore in our small boat and land him on Southend pier so that he could telephone London and report the disasters which had overtaken him and had resulted in no filming at all. He came back an hour later in a hired launch and announced that everyone was to return to London except Charles de Jaegar and Johnny Ray, who would continue to operate with the hand camera. If the weather improved, we were to proceed to Harwich and Pin Mill, where they would rejoin us with a couple of staff cars. So we were left in peace to cook a welcome evening meal, after which the cheerful Johnny established himself in a forecastle bunk and poor Charles reclined, none too comfortably, with the gash bucket as a footrest, the bunk being rather too short for him. He suffered in silence, as well he might, having been brought to this seafaring assignment from a luxurious hotel in the Middle East. A camera man's life must be one of great contrasts.

That night the north-easter died away. Just before daybreak I sensed a different motion in the barge and on poking my head out of of the cabin scuttle-hatch, saw the "bob" on our masthead fluttering feebly to a light westerly breeze. It was up anchor and away, and we called our camera men for pints of

Chris Chataway and the author aboard the *Cambria*.

tea and bacon and eggs. Everything went right for us — warm sunshine and a smooth sea, as we ambled down the West Swin under all light weather canvas. Charles picked out suitable shots for Johnny to take, sometimes stretching himself on deck to read a book and doze. He even took an afternoon nap in his gash-bucket bunk.

We anchored in the early evening off Pin Mill, in the River Orwell. The B.B.C. car soon appeared at the top of the landing Hard, outside the *Butt and Oyster Inn*. Stephen Hearst was the first to greet us as we stepped ashore from our small boat. Everything was organised and arranged. In the morning the *Cambria* was to sail up and down Butterman's Bay (the longest reach in the Orwell) and I would point out to Chris Chataway such interesting features of London River as he might question me about. The fact that it was the Orwell and not London River would not matter in the film as long as Charles de Jaegar (restored to his repaired sound-vision box) and Johnny Ray kept the shore line out of shot. As I steered, Chris Chataway was to interview me in the wheelhouse. And in due course this was done without any more disasters.

There was, however, one more memorable hour in filming this adventure. Chataway needed a training run to keep in running trim before his serious training for the Olympics. Could I suggest a four or five mile cross-country route to stretch his legs.

"Yes — across Woolverstone Park. I'll come with you."

He was rather taken aback by this offer, but I took him along to my cottage to change and, to his astonishment, showed him a bronze medal I had won in the A.A.A. Marathon championship years before, from Windsor to Stamford Bridge, 26 miles 285 yards. He simply could not believe that a beer-drinking barge skipper could run!

We duly set off across country, to the amazement of the villagers, and when I ran out of puff I would direct him to some far clump of trees and cut the corners off to pick him up again. The way he moved his legs put me in mind of a young deer. He was, of course, much too fast for me until we finally came to the top of a hill which led down to my cottage. I knew there was not far to go now and I scampered away in front of him down the hill.

"Not too fast — not too fast" he said, thinking we had yet a long way to go. But I dived through a gap in the hedge, over a fence and was indoors while he went careering off down to the river. It was a great moment (for me!) when Chataway said I was going too fast.

In the *Butt and Oyster* I revived myself with several pints of stout and Chataway looked at me incredulously. "You might even have been in the Olympic Games yourself," he said "if you had been a few minutes faster in your Marathon."

Next day, the filming completed, we set sail for the Humber for a cargo of coal to be loaded at Keadby, up the Trent. Stephen Hearst and his men set off by car for Bradwell to interview the last professional wildfowler in Essex, Bill Linnet. He lived alone away on the marshes near the ancient Saxon church of St. Peter's-on-the-Wall, in a tiny wooden cottage which had once served as a Customs and Excise outpost. If ever a man lived a simple life it was Bill Linnet. He was up before dawn and abed by sunset. Punt and gun were his only tools and he lived by the wildfowl that fell to him. Yet even he, living out there by the desolate tidal marshes, once came into big money by way of a reward. I do not know if he ever collected it. He was poling and paddling round the creeks and ditches at dawn and noticed, more than once, an unfamiliar object in the reeds. He rowed in to investigate and it proved to be the mutilated torso of a man murdered in London. The police had been searching for it for a long time, but, of course, Bill never saw any newspapers.

The film ''Away from it All'' was in time expertly produced and was acclaimed not only in Britain but in many parts of the world. Letters of appreciation flooded in from Australia, New Zealand and America.

I was paid £50 by an appreciative B.B.C.

Model of *Cambria* sailing on the Round Pond, London.

CHAPTER SEVENTEEN

On Fire At Sea

The nearest I came to drowning
Was under a North Sea wave.
I sailed at ten
With two brave men
But one we could not save.

THE *Gowan Brae* was a 67 foot twin engined yacht which had once served as an R.A.F. rescue launch. Her owner was a brawny Scotsman, and an engineer like so many of his countrymen, and, to cap it all, he rejoiced in the name of Douggie Burns. He walked like a man accustomed to a kilt. He ought never to have worn English trousers.

His little ship had been on charter to Dutchmen in Holland as a holiday cruiser and the time had come to bring her home. Would I go across to the Hook of Holland and fetch her to Harwich? Douggie would act as engineer, my knowledge of mechanics being very poor, and an old wartime friend of his, Colonel Tibb, would sail as cook. "Tibby" as we called him, had come to England with the Australian Army in the First World War — 1914-1918. He claimed descent from an old Norfolk family who lived in and around the village of Tibenham. He never went back to Australia and remained here as Douggie's bosom pal. They were two battle-tried men of high courage and when we faced disaster on that brief voyage in the *Gowan Brae* I felt privileged to face danger with such men as these.

While my barge was temporarily laid up Tibby and I crossed over on the Harwich—Hook-of-Holland ferry, Douggie being already in Holland to take delivery of his ship. They relied on me as the only sailorman of the party. We found her moored in a small basin near the Hook and Douggie had the two Crossley diesels ready for sea. "We're ready to go" he said as we stepped aboard. But the weather glass was low and a south west gale blowing so I advised delaying the start of the voyage until things looked brighter. There was a heavy swell breaking at the mouth of the waterway. Tibby's niece, Olive, was aboard, but, like the sensible Lancashire lass she was, she agreed to go home by packet boat rather than come in the *Gowan Brae*. What a blessing that decision turned out to be. "Take care of Tibby. His heart is bad and he'll be 70 tomorrow" were her last words to me before she boarded the Harwich packet.

I looked over the ship and, being a sailorman of some 25 years experience at the time and subject to all the old instincts and superstitions, I did not like her. Her wooden decks were sodden with oil. There were oil drums lashed all over the place. The housing chocks for the lifeboat were over the engine room — there was no other place to put her. The lifeboat was also full of oil drums, and a can of petrol for the generator, and various bits of rope and equipment which would have made it impossible to launch her. I had all this cleared out and lashed her down in a more seamanlike manner than the way the Dutchmen had left her.

Having cleared the decks of lumber, I felt there was not much more I could do in the way of preparation. But still I did not like her. She was not my idea of a sea-going vessel, but Douggie assured me that the engines were in good trim and would give her a good 15 knots. She had a short mast but no sail of any sort. I resigned myself, somewhat reluctantly, to trusting implicitly in the engines and Douggie's undoubted ability as an engineer.

As soon as the barometer started to rise and the thunder of the breakers on the sea wall died down I decided to make a start. Surely at 15 knots it could only be a day's passage. What was 120 miles at 15 knots, even in a doubtful ship?

Outside, the heavy swell over the uneven sea-bottom made the *Gowan Brae* roll abominally. Tibby was soon seasick and so was Douggie to a lesser degree. But the swell was smooth-topped and I asked Douggie to "give her all she's got." He did, but the power was too much for the ship and I had to ease her down and alter course a little now and then to reduce the excessive rolling. Tibby came up to the wheelhouse with a mug of tea, offering to give me a spell at the wheel, trying hard to muffle his retching. But he was no seaman and the best service he could be was to call out Douggie to check the engines and turn in himself. Douggie came struggling forward and reported that both engines were O.K. for the time being, but one of them needed looking at later. He stayed with me in the wheelhouse and for short periods gave me a rest from steering. We were making good progress and I reckoned we would be in Harwich the next day. It was only the smell of the engine room which had made Douggie feel seasick: "I feel better now. I'll go and see if there is anything wrong with that starboard engine."

I took the wheel and he disappeared aft. Presently I heard a shout and, looking astern, I saw smoke coming from the engine room port holes. Knowing that diesel engines sometimes give off black smoke if the injectors are not working properly, I took no notice until Douggie came stumbling along the deck in a state of great alarm.

"We're on fire!"

I pulled the little fire-extinguisher off the wheelhouse bulkhead and said, as calmly as I could: "Take this and call Tibby."

Tibby was sleeping abaft the engine room and would be trapped if there was a serious conflagration. That was the first priority — to get Tibby out. By the time the old fellow got on deck and Douggie started to use the fire extinguisher, flames were coming out of the portholes and in a matter of seconds the whole of the mid-ship section of the ship was a mass of roaring flames. It was too late to hope that a single fire extinguisher would put out such a blaze, and the others were down in the engine room. The engines were slowly thumping to a stop, but while the ship still had way on I put Tibby at the wheel and rushed aft to try to launch the lifeboat. As Douggie and I tried to heave her off the engine room deckhead, flames shot up round us and I could see that the boat's bottom was burnt through. By now the ship had lost way. "What shall we do?" Douggie shouted, for the fire was roaring with a deafening noise.

"The wind is west, tide ebbing. We must let go the anchor with all the chain you have and try to hold her head to wind to keep the fire from coming forrard."

Down went the anchor and we gave her 60 fathoms of chain. I watched it stream out ahead as the *Gowan Brae* rolled sluggishly to the tide and I knew the anchor had reached the bottom of the North Sea, even if it was not holding very well. The ship came round and rode to it nearly, but not quite, head to wind.

The flames and sparks were reaching up everywhere amidships, Tibby said, "Where are the distress flares?" I shook my head and pointed aft. The *Gowan Brae* was making her own flares which must have been visible for miles. I was shocked by the fearsome rapidity with which the fire spread, and the noise was so deafening that we had to shout to each other. The heat became overpowering and drove us out of the wheelhouse and on to the fore-deck. We looked like being roasted alive.

I had an old blue Merchant Service mackintosh and this we held up to keep off the intense heat of the fire. We crouched there for what seemed an interminable time, hoping the fire might die down. But it grew worse and the roar was frightening. All this time I was trying to think of some way of saving our lives if no ship should come to us. And there was none visible. It was a dark night, lit only by the *Gowan Brae*. One forlorn hope was that when the ship burned to the waterline the sea would break in, put out the fire and leave us with enough wreckage to hold on to until help came.

Then came an alarming discovery. A glow came up from a deck light and I could see that the fire was spreading forward below decks. Everything seemed red hot. It was obvious that very soon the bit of foredeck where we were standing was going to cave in and precipitate us into a quick and painful cremation. Douggie and Tibby managed to laugh about it. "I've got all that bacon in the galley and now we're getting fried ourselves." "I don't fancy you for breakfast, Tibby," Douglas said. "I'll bet you'd be all bloody rind."

There was no panic with these men. "We've got to slide down that chain and hang on to it. This deck is going," I said. "Get your life-belts round you and get into the water."

Douggie said, "I'll go first, then Tibby, then you. We can hold him between us." I agreed. "Take care of Tibby," the niece had said, and this was uppermost in our minds. Douggie edged his body over the rail and went down the anchor chain hand over hand. Once he was in the water he got a good grip on the chain, leaving his left arm free to help Tibby. The old man struggled over the side, gripping the chain tightly with both hands as a heavy swell swung his legs out horizontally. As they streamed out in the fast running tide, the lifebelt slipped down off his body, down his legs, and floated away into the darkness.

"Tibby's lost his lifebelt." Douggie shouted.

I handed him down mine and Tibby got his head and one arm through it.

"Come on, Bob" Douggie shouted. "Three of us can hold on to two lifebelts."

I slid down the chain holding on to it with one hand and resting the other on Tibby's lifebelt. The three of us hung on thus for probably an hour. Tibby was shivering and his face was purple. Periodically a big swell would dash us against the bows of the ship.

The two survivors from the blazing *Gowan Brae*, Douggie Burns and the author.

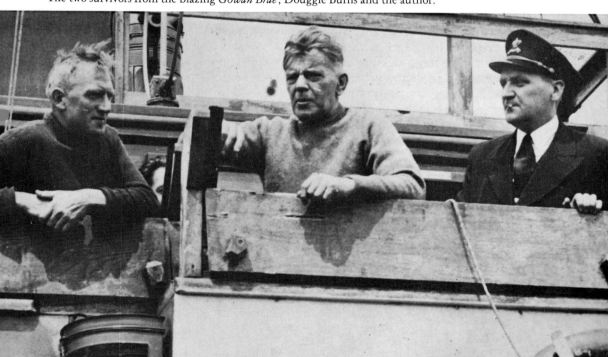

Close to us, in the glare of the blaze, a yellow oil drum came floating by. Douggie shouted "I'll get it for you," knowing I had no lifebelt. Without a second's hesitation he let go of the chain and struck out. I yelled "No" but it was too late. At that moment I was washed by a breaking wave on to the wrong side of the stem so that I could not see what happened, but when I was able to haul myself round again Douggie had disappeared into the darkness. He had not realised that the North Sea tides can run hard. I heard a faint shout in the distance but that was all. I was convinced that we should never see him again. Tibby gasped, "Douggie's gone."

I do not know how long Tibby and I hung on there. It might have been an hour, may be much longer. I had my arms right round him most of the time so that I had both hands gripping the chain. But he was a bit bulky with his overcoat on and as the burning bows rose and fell to a particularly heavy swell, my right hand grip failed and I was dashed to the starboard side and Tibby round to the port side. As we collided again I rose up on a wave and saw the masthead lights of a ship. She was a long way away; about five miles, I guessed.

"Hang on, Tibby. There's a ship coming ", I shouted in his ear. But I lied to him because I could tell from the angle of her lights that she was not coming our way. There was no hope. Tibby, breathless and distressed, said, "To hell with this. I can't stand this cold any longer. I'm getting back up there."

"Hang on. Hang on. There's a ship coming."

He tried to get up the anchor chain hand over hand, lost his grip and fell back into the sea out of my reach. Before he disappeared I caught a glimpse of his bald head. He was face down. I let go the chain and tried to swim after him, but I was on the lee side. Burning oil was on the water and the mast had collapsed, all afire, so that I had to swim out round it and then turn myself head to tide hoping to sight Tibby. I am a poor swimmer and the tide was carrying me further and further away from the stern of the ship. I got outside the ring of the glow and it was very dark. There was no sign of Tibby. I paddled away with a breast stroke, convinced now that I was the only one left alive.

I seemed to be sinking deeper and deeper and swallowing more and more sea water. Perhaps I was slowly drowning. I called out the names of my two little girls. "Anne . . . little Jill", I heard myself saying, as though it was someone else's voice. It was hollow and eerie and not my voice at all. But even then the instinct of self-preservation was strong enough to make me wonder if I could swim far enough to get into the shipping lane, or even to the Belgian coast 60 miles away.

Then there was a big explosion aboard the *Gowan Brae*, now some distance away, and a greater glow extended over the sea as far as where I was feebly swimming. In that sudden glow, I saw, some 25 yards away from me, a lifebelt. I struggled towards it, grabbed it and ducked my head and arms through it so that it buoyed me up from the armpits. I was so relieved, I felt as good as saved, although by then the blazing ship seemed to be no more than a bonfire in the distance. Every time I rose on to the crest of a wave I gazed round for a ship, but there was none; only blackness. I had no idea how long it would be until daylight.

Once I heard a rushing noise behind me, and thinking it was a big breaking wave coming, I looked round and saw, to my amazement, a green light. It was a ship!

I yelled ''Help, Help.'' as loud as I could and a searchlight swept across the water. I heard a voice say ''Backboard, backboard.'' I kept shouting. The searchlight swept round and I heard men shouting in Dutch. At last the searchlight settled on me and heaving lines came flying over. I grabbed one and quickly wound it round my wrist. My fingers were too numb to grip it. I could see the ship now and slowly I was drawn towards it. There was a rope ladder over the side. A hefty young Dutch lad came down the ladder and grabbed me firmly round the waist as I was washed against the ship's side. He had a strong arm and rung by rung we struggled up to the ship's rail. Hands reached out and hove me over the bulwarks and on to the deck in a heap. I got to my feet. ''There is another man near here;'' then I fell to being sick, bringing up a most unpleasant mixture of salt water and oil. The captain came off the bridge and I told him that Tibby must be in the tide-line astern of the burning wreck. He nodded, and I was carted off to the galley. The young Dutchman who had helped me up the ladder sat me on a bench in front of the cooking stove and stripped off my clothes. With his great warm hands he rubbed my body and put his arms around me to try to stop my shivering. Other membes of the crew came in now and then to tell me that they were looking for ''the other man''. My brawny Dutch ''nurse'' warmed some blankets and wrapped them round me as gently as any woman. He made me a mug of hot coffee. Still there was no news of Tibby and I went out on deck and yelled his name several times. There was no answer. I was led back to the galley.

Presently the Captain came in. He spoke good English. ''We do not find any man here, but we think we hear something a little way away so we are under way to go and see.''

The next thing I remember was looking up as the galley door opened and there stood Douggie, haggard and cramped, supported by two seamen.

''Where's Tibby?''

I shook my head. He slumped down and they started to dry him out as I had been. We did not talk, but went out on deck in the vain hope that we might see or hear poor Tibby. After a time we were urged to go below where two bunks had been prepared for us. The Master, Captain J. Van der Zwan, came down and told us that he had sent out a radio distress call and now he had three other ships stationed strategically round the area. They were bigger ships and better to able to find any other survivors in the water. They were to remain on ''search

The old isolation hospital which laid afloat in Long Reach, River Thames.

and rescue'' station until after daybreak. In the meantime our ship would proceed on her voyage to Amsterdam.

She was the Dutch coaster *Tyro*, loaded with coal from Cardiff. When they first sighted us, the captain said, he thought we were a Belgian fishing boat with a brazier, such as they used to carry amidships for cooking shellfish. But when his seamen reported high flames and sparks flying into the air, he decided to alter course and investigate. It was little short of a miracle that they should find me in the dark, just a head bobbing about in the waves a long way from the burning *Gowan Brae*. I realised, too, that the Captain had manoevred the *Tyro* as close to me as possible in such a manner that there was least risk of my being injured or killed by the propellor, or had my bones broken against the side of the ship. Feats of seamanship are something I have always admired and I had every reason to admire the skill of this Dutchman.

Douggie and I slept like logs until after daybreak. When we woke the cook came to us. ''We are very sorry we cannot give you an English breakfast. We have no bacon.'' But would we mind having steak and eggs!! Would we mind!

Starved of bacon and meat through six years of war and severely rationed for another five years after by a Socialist government, Douggie and I lined up at the mess table and regarded our plates of beautifully cooked beef steaks with eggs sizzling on the top with nothing short of amazement. We had not seen anything like it for many a day.

Because these Dutchmen saved my life, and Douggie's too, and treated us with such kindness and consideration aboard their ship, I have listed their names here in the hope that if any read this book, they will write to me.

Captain	J. Van der Zwan	Vlaardingen
First Mate	W. G. J. Van Zelm van Eldik	Rotterdam
Second Mate	J. F. Boogerd	Den Haag
Chief Engineer	J. Kenter	Rotterdam
Second Engineer	A. C. Wiltschut	Rotterdam
Assistant Engineer	W. M. Mulder	Schiedam
Cook	J. M. Van Beers	Rotterdam
Second Cook	A. Dekker	Delft
Able Seaman	A. Spaans	Den Haag
Able Seaman	P. Bruggeling	Den Haag
Deckhand	G. Van Tol	Rotterdam
Deckhand	G. Van Luytelaar	Soest

Their names were sent to me on request by the owners, N. V. Maatschappij Zeevaart of Rotterdam, with a modest little note saying "We are very pleased that one our vessels has had the opportunity to give you this assistance."

The *Tyro* landed us in lovely Amsterdam, which was my favourite city — and I was never a city lover. Amsterdam with its avenues and canals, its friendly people and pleasant cafes, was to me a sort of dream city. It has changed now. Strange people of all colours and creeds flooding the streets and cafes have taken away its "Dutchness." I pray that one day Amsterdam will be its old self again — stable, historic and hospitable.

We shook hands with all the crew before stepping ashore. Each wished us good luck and Captain Van der Zwan said: "I am sorry we could not have saved your friend. The other ships have not found him. The *Gowan Brae* burned to the waterline and then sank."

The British Consul arranged our passage home and we took the packet boat to Harwich. The press were there to greet us, but it was a local East Anglian paper which summed up our experience in the headline "It was Roast or Drown".

It is only by something akin to a miracle that I am able to sit in my old stone cottage in the Isle of Wight, looking out over the Solent waters, to write these lines thirty odd years later.

During those thirty years I inquired for Captain Van der Zwan in every Dutch port I visited, especially when I traded in the *Vectis Isle* to many small inland ports up the canals and rivers of the Netherlands. In the big ports like Amsterdam and Rotterdam I always asked our local shipping agents if they knew of his whereabouts but they would shake their heads and tell me that there was a new *Tyro* and that the old *Tyro* had "gone". And of the Captain who saved my life they knew nothing.

It was almost thirty years to the day when a Captain Willem Wester of the Carisbrooke Shipping Company of the Isle of Wight, who was having a drink in my cottage, said: "I think I can find him for you." Telex messages were flashed to and fro and at last I was put in touch with a Captain J. Van der Zwan, a retired captain living in the village of Brielle, not far from Rotterdam. Letters were exchanged and he immediately took ship from the Hook of Holland to Harwich. I waited for him on Ryde Pier and there he was, standing on the stern of the ferry boat as she berthed. Although we had only seen each other once, thirty years before, on the night of the rescue, we recognised each other immediately and he and his wife spent the weekend at St. Anne's Cottage. It was a merry re-union with Dutch and Island friends making up what my wife called a Thanksgiving Dinner.

Captain Van der Zwan, the man who saved my life, retired in his home near Rotterdam with his wife. We met again thirty years later on the Isle of Wight.

CHAPTER EIGHTEEN

A Sailor Ashore

A SAILORMAN, especially one in the Coastwise and Home Trade, meets a far greater variety of people than would a person living and working on shore. The "home-every-night" man, in the course of his daily task, meets and talks with the same sort of people day in, day out, often year in, year out, to the end of his active life. The seafarer faces a different scene, talks to different people, and comes into contact with all sorts of customs and traditions every time he sets foot on dry land. And the average honest citizen finds more interest in talk about ships and seamen than in the humdrum conversation of his humdrum neighbours.

Taking cargoes of barley to Snape Maltings up the River Alde in Suffolk, I once stepped ashore and walked up to neighbouring Blaxhall to try a pint in the *Ship Inn*. As I opened the door I saw as merry a scene as I could ever wish to see, even though Blaxhall is literally miles from anywhere. There in the corner sat a villager playing a lively tune on an old fashioned melodeon. On the floor of the bar four couples were dancing, opposite each other, the ancient taps and steps of a hundred years ago. In subsequent voyages to that place I got to know their names. There was Eli, a farm hand with feet like a fairy, who could out-dance any man or woman for miles around (and out-fight any stranger who interrupted) and "Strawberry", who, I felt sure, could dance any woman off the stage in London's West End. Another hefty young chap who went by the name of "Jumbo" clumped away in perfect time, never missing a step or sequence. They were a fine crowd and in spite of the fact that their dances required a great deal of wind and energy, they could have danced all night if the ale was forthcoming.

At the head of a trestle table sat a broad shouldered man with a face that exuded good humour, known as "Wickets" Richards. Well respected, he kept good order in the house and called for a dance or a song as he thought fit. And if it was to be a song he would thump the table with his ale pot and roar "Singer's on his feet". Every one would fall silent and there was no question of anyone talking or interrupting while the song was sung. The songs they sang were a hundred to two hundred years old, sometimes with a chorus they would all know. Bob Scase, 80 odd years of age, would be called upon for his favourite item "Death of General Wolfe" and he would sing it with such vigour and

Above. On the left Fred Lapslie, former mate of the *Cambria*.
Right is Dick Durham from Leigh-on-Sea, the last man to serve as mate in a genuine working barge under sail.

Below. Left the author aboard *Vectis Isle* for the last eight years of a seafaring life under sail. Right Henry Trefusis, a valuable shipmate over many years, aboard *Vectis Isle*, with Ernie Young (left) the engineer-mate.

conviction that one could imagine that he must have been in the battle of Quebec himself.

A black-haired, high-cheekboned woman — a handsome Romany — sang "The Yellow Handkerchief" and, although middle-aged, danced as lightly as any of the youngsters. Her name was Phoebe Smith and her husband Joe could play his fiddle by holding the bow between his knees and playing the violin on the bow. They had a dark haired daughter, also named Phoebe, with long flashing earrings, who could dance like her mother, once persuaded to cast off her shyness.

Phoebe Smith told me that she had been born and brought up in a caravan. Her father played the fiddle and taught her the steps. "He was forever telling me to 'pick my feet up' and one day he set off for market saying 'I'll bring you back a pair of dancing shoes to make you pick your feet up'. I expected to be given golden slippers, but he came back with a heavy pair of hob-nailed boots. 'They'll make you pick your feet up' he said. And I had to dance in those hob nails for weeks on the wooden floor of the caravan: but they *did* teach me to pick my feet up!"

I had to keep my end up by singing "When the wind blows our barge will go". They soon picked it up and sang it for years after on their "song and dance nights".

Cyril Poacher, his cap askew over a lean, weathered face, nearly always sang "The Nutting Song" and there was a young man with a ruddy complexion, fair hair and blue eyes who could be heard in the next parish when he rendered "The Organist". That was probably the nearest *Blaxhall Ship* got to modern music.

For a sailor ashore, they were lively and memorable days. If we were discharging cargo in Poole about Maytime I used to borrow a bike and pedal out to the village of Hampreston to see the schoolchildren carrying their freshly cut Maypole to the church meadow and singing sweet little rhymes which I could not remember. If I was lucky I might be able to stay long enough to see them dancing round the gaily decorated pole chanting verses their grandmothers had taught them. The church, the meadow and the quaint little school are still there; and will be for evermore — I hope.

When I sailed a handsome old ketch-barge named the *Martinet* we used to take cattle cake from London to Wells in Norfolk, a difficult port to negotiate, but the trial and anxiety of getting over the sand bar was rewarded by the delightful people we met ashore. Whatever function was in progress we bargemen were always welcomed in, be it a dance, an outing or a carnival procession. One of their favourite songs in the evening was "The Old Ram of Derbyshire", the words of which cannot be repeated here. While discharging at Wells an old man with two collie dogs came and watched us. One of the local chaps unloading us said to me:— "Do you know who that is? That's the skipper of the *Cutty Sark*, Captain Woodgett.'' I walked along the deck hoping to be able to speak with such a famous seaman, but he looked meaningly aloft to where we had a broken ratline hanging in the main rigging. Before I could greet him he turned his back on me and walked away — in disgust, I believe. I went aloft and spliced a new one immediately. But at least I had seen the famous Captain and he had deigned to *look* at my ship. I was sorry about that ratline.

Hearing and seeing the traditional songs, ceremonies and dances in out of the way ''village ports'' encouraged me to find out more about them. Eventually the Kennedy family, of the English Folk Dance and Song Society, gave me opportunities to trace the origin of songs I had heard and many that I had learned from my father, who could sing all day and play the melodeon, concertina, violin, piano, piccolo and the church organ.

Before the days of newspapers, news was carried from place to place by horse and foot, hill-top signals, pre-arranged bonfires and town criers. But even after newspapers became quite commonplace there were large sections of the population who could neither read nor write. So to many, news of current events was brought by the ballad singer, who could buy a broadsheet from a street seller, put what tune he liked to it, and sing it for a pot of ale or a hat full of coppers. Thus was born what are now known as Broadsheet Ballads. Many have been salvaged, collected and published in book form.

The industrious ballad writers seized on any subject under the sun — battles, murder, rape, miracles and even local scandal. (Present day law of libel could probably have had most of them in court for the lines they composed.)

Penny, the *Cambria*'s dog was trained to call the mate. ''Wakey, Wakey, Mr Mate''.

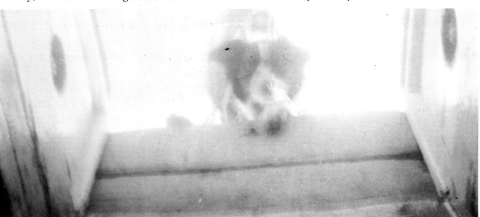

Here's an East Anglian sample of comparatively recent times, 1876, the year my mother was born. It is a long sheet of paper, ten inches wide, and is headed:—

MURDER AT CAMBRIDGE

Robert Brown stands charged with the murder of Emma Rolfe, by cutting her throat with a razor, on a Common near Cambridge on Thursday night, August 28th 1876. The prisoner has confessed the crime to Police Constable Wheel.

(Now comes the ballad, entitled the "Unfortunate Girl.")

In the quiet town of Cambridge the deed has been done
That I'm sure has surprised and startled each one
An unfortunate woman but just in her prime
Alas is the victim of this cruel crime.

Well known in Cambridge, from virtue betrayed
In the path of dishonour too early she strayed
But whatever she's been we can all understand
Her life was as sweet as the best in the land.

Poor Emma Rolfe had no time to repent
On Midsummer Common to Eternity went
Robert Brown was her murderer, in prison he's cast
From virtue she strayed to be murdered at last.

A policeman was brought and the murderer confessed
For the crime he committed he now has no rest
He would give all the world to recall that sad hour
But what has been done is beyond earthly power.

She was murdered that night with her sins on her head
I hope they're forgiven now she's laying dead
Though lost to this world, despised and forlorn
Someone will miss the poor girl now she's gone.

Robert Brown will be tried for this unmanly crime
And if he's found guilty must suffer in time
We pity his brother, relations as well
Who are grieving for him as he lies in his cell.

His poor victim lies in her cold narrow bed
Never no more to her ruin be led
Young girls, beware you are not led astray
For plenty will quickly decoy you away.

133

There you have the whole story — although what would happen to the ballad writer in the case of Robert Brown being found not guilty, I would not care to imagine! Of course, news like the death of Nelson or the battle of Waterloo produced a veritable flood of broadsheet ballads.

Pleasant days ashore took much of the hardness out of life under sail. I met people I would never have met had I led a quieter life on land, or scrambled into the money-grubbing "rat-race".

        *   *   *   *   *   *   *

Inevitably, the time came when sail was no longer an economic proposition. Such vessels were hated by dockers who had to load them, ridiculed by lockmen in the Port of London, and doubted by a new generation of merchants and agents who knew nothing about them. People who came into the trade could only conceive delivery by train or by lorry. Transport costs rocketed. We could still carry bulk cargoes at less than a third of their costs. At one time cargo by coastal seas worked out at one penny per ton per mile cheaper than movement by any other means. As owner of the *Cambria* I struggled to convince business people that they could still move their goods cheaply and swiftly by sailing barge. But I was "punching the tide" and although everyone was very polite, we swung round the buoy for up to three weeks at a time without earning a penny. When we did get a freight, dockers were resentful, and even insulting, about the work of stowing cargo in our hold. Instead of using every available cubic foot in the barge they would "draw the slings" and topple it in anyhow. If the barge was thus badly loaded so that she was not in a fit trim to go to sea, the mate and I would slog for hours and hours, after they had gone home, shifting and re-stowing hundreds of heavy bags for our own safety and for the safety of the cargo entrusted to us. It was heartbreaking to say the least of it; but still we carried on and mates like Ginger Latham of London and Dick Durham from Leigh backed me up manfully, even though there was little monetary reward.

One day I was visited by certain eminent personalities who had formed the new Maritime Trust to preserve and put on display ships and equipment of interest and importance in the commercial history of this country. The President was H.R.H. the Duke of Edinburgh, ably backed by a chairman in the Duke of Westminster. Director of the Ships committee was Vice-Admiral Sir Patrick Bayly, and Captain R. C. C. Greenlees served as Secretary. If the *Cambria* could not earn a living in the modern world they would purchase her, maintain her in good order and put her on show as the last real working sailing barge. To this I agreed. It was better than letting her get into the hands of foolish romantics, although several other old barges suffered that fate.

So *Cambria* ended her life as she had begun it, a link in Britain's commerce; and she was the last purely sailing vessel to trade under the Red Ensign.

Being a seaman by trade and unwilling to swallow the anchor, I cast around for a small power vessel to compete on my own. I finally bought a pretty little Dutch built ship from the Isle of Wight, called the *Vectis Isle*: and until I had passed my allotted three score years and ten, I pushed and pioneered into the Continental trade, from small ports in England to the inland waterways of Holland, Belgium, and France. Life changed — but I was still at sea for a living. And in a small ship like the *Vectis Isle* carrying 260 tons of cargo, a breeze for a bargeman was still a breeze for me.

Cambria in her retirement berth at Upnor with the Training Ship *Arethusa* at her moorings in the Medway.

The End. Owners had their crack barges broken up rather than let them fall into the hands of unskilful amateurs.

Above the breaking up of the *Sara* proved harder than these men at Greenhithe expected. Below the end of the lovely *Dreadnought*.